D0916020

THE ECLOGUES

OF VIRGIL

THE
ECLOGUES
OF VIRGIL

A TRANSLATION BY

DAVID FERRY

FARRAR, STRAUS AND GIROUX

NEW YORK

Library of Congress Cataloging-in-Publication Data
Virgil.
 [Bucolica. English & Latin]
 The eclogues of Virgil : a translation / by David Ferry. — 1st
ed.
 p. cm.
 ISBN 0-374-14634-9 (alk. paper)
 1. Pastoral poetry, Latin—Translations into English. 2. Country
life—Rome—Poetry. I. Ferry, David. II. Title.
PA6807.B7F47 1999
871´.01—dc21 *98-52547*

Some of these eclogues have previously appeared in
Agni, Arion, Literary Imagination, Persephone,
Raritan, *and* The Threepenny Review.

This book is dedicated to the memory of

ELIZABETH FERRY CHAFFEE

PENELOPE FERRY SMITH

BERNICE FRANCES DAVIDSON

Contents

Introduction

Meliboeus has been dispossessed of his pastures and Tityrus has been put into possession of his, and sits contentedly under a beech tree playing his pipe.

Another shepherd, Corydon, alone in the noontime midsummer heat, hopelessly in love with a beautiful boy, sings of his love with confused ridiculous convincing passion.

Menalcas and Damoetas, rubes, quarrel furiously and hilariously, and then compete in songs of love, and riddles, and work songs, and Palaemon, their neighbor, declares their singing contest a tie.

The poet offers a charming birthday gift to a newborn child. The gift is immense, a prophecy that the child will preside over a new golden age and a new society, in which there will be no war, no labor, no sorrow.

Mopsus and Menalcas, with exquisite mutual courtesy, take turns singing about the shepherd Daphnis, first about his death and its bad consequences for the crops and then about his apotheosis and how there will be offerings to him, blessing the fields.

A drunken satyr, Silenus, the tutor of Bacchus, god of wine and song, having been playfully tied up with his own garlands by two boys and a water nymph, sings the songs he had promised them he would sing: stories, among others, of the beginning of the world, the love of Pasiphaë for a bull, the violent murderous story of Procne, the story of Scylla the whirlpool drowning the Ithacan sailors, and the story of the calling of Gallus, an actual poet and important figure in Virgil's world of literature and politics, to be a poet under the sign of Hesiod and Linus.

Daphnis, maybe the same Daphnis, maybe not, calls Meliboeus, who maybe is or maybe is not the same Meliboeus, to hear a singing contest between the Arcadian shepherds Thyrsis and Corydon, and Corydon, who may or may not be the same Corydon, is declared the victor, though it is hard to see why, both songs being so compellingly beautiful. But Corydon's is the sweeter.

Damon, at the brink—or, in his song, as if at the brink—of suicide, sings of Nysa's abandonment of him, and of her marriage to Mopsus. Alphesiboeus sings a contending song, as if in the voice of a woman who loves Daphnis and casts spells to bring him back to her. Perhaps Daphnis does return or perhaps she deludes herself.

Moeris and Lycidas are going to town. Evening is coming on, and perhaps a rainstorm is coming as well. One of them has been dispossessed of the ownership of his land. The shepherd Menalcas (surely not the clown Menalcas?) had promised to hold their world together with his music. "But what can music do / Against the weapons of soldiers?" Moeris and Lycidas, as they journey toward town, past the tomb of still another shepherd, are remembering and yet forgetting their songs.

Gallus is heard lamenting Lycoris's desertion of him. He says, as his song comes to an end, "now farewell, Nymphs; / No longer do our songs give pleasure now; / Farewell to the groves." And the poet of the Eclogues echoes him: "Go home, my full-fed goats, you've eaten your fill, / The Evening Star is rising; it's time to go home."

Wendell Clausen says that "not only did Virgil compose the *Eclogues,* he also, and to some extent simultaneously, composed the Book of *Eclogues,* a poetic achievement scarcely less remarkable . . . [In] Virgil's book the design of individual poems has been adjusted to the design of the book as a whole."[1] Many scholars have discussed the nature of this design and have interpreted its meanings (and responded to its pleasures) in different ways, and it is remarkable how the book has sustained and nourished multifarious interpretations and resolved and pacified them with its harmonies. Not resolved, really, or pacified, but, in Paul Alpers's term, "suspended" them "in the harmonies of verse."[2]

The Eclogues are a book in ways that are obvious and not so obvious. Eclogue IX, almost at the end of the series, clearly echoes Eclogue I and sadly completes it, as the shepherds, dispossessed like Meliboeus,

journey to the town, and the songs are being forgotten. Eclogues II, VIII, and X tell versions of the same erotic story, of abandonment and longing, and each one says hard things about the implacability of love and love's cruelty: "Each creature is led by that which it most longs for"; "I know what Love is . . . Love / Is not of our blood and he is not of our kind"; "what could teach the god of love to pity? . . . Love conquers all, and all must yield to Love." Eclogues VII and III are alike in being singing contests, and V is a contest too, uncontentiously, and all three of them sing about, among other things, the hardness of labor in the fields and vineyards and the precariousness of the shepherd's and cowherd's life: "The field is dry; in the blighted air the grass / Is dying for lack of water; Bacchus denies / The shade of his vines to the arid hill"; "Round up the sheep, boys, find the cool of the shade; / This heat will dry the milk up in the udders . . . My flock is skin and bones, and it isn't for love; / The evil eye is on my lambs. But whose?"; "Apollo has left our fields, and Pales too. / In the furrows where we hopefully planted barley, / Darnel and tares and sterile oat-grass grow." Eclogues IV and VI invoke the Muses, and each, in its own way, goes out beyond (while still remaining within) the limiting fiction of pastoral song. Clearly their occurrence at the center of the sequence, along with the sublime apotheosis in V, is a significant feature of our experience of the shape of the book.

There are patterns, too, of political attitudes, attitudes toward power, and specifically toward the Julian house, the house of Julius Caesar and Octavian (Augustus). In Eclogue I there is Tityrus's gratitude to Octavian for his land, in tension with Meliboeus's having been unpropertied so that it could be given to Octavian's veterans. Meliboeus says bitterly: "This is what civil war has brought down upon us. / So Meliboeus, carefully set out / Your plants and pear trees, all in rows—for whom? / For strangers, for others, we have farmed our land." In Eclogue V it may be that one way (though only one way) to read Daphnis's death is to think of the death of Julius Caesar, and in Eclogue IX one of the half-forgotten, half-remembered songs predicts the rising of Julius Caesar's star in the sky: "Venus's grandson Caesar's star is rising . . . / The star that brings such joy to the ripening grain . . . / Daphnis, plant your pear trees . . . years from now / The children of your children will gather the pears."

That this is a book is implicated in every expression of the opening passage of Eclogue VII:

Daphnis, one day, was sitting in the shade
Of a murmuring ilex tree, and Corydon
And Thyrsis, both nearby, were tending their flocks,
Thyrsis his sheep and Corydon his she-goats,
Their udders swollen with milk. Thyrsis and he
Were both like flowers in bloom, the two of them,
Arcadians both, and ready to compete
With song replying to song replying to song.
And I was a little way off, mulching the roots
Of my myrtle plants to keep them from the cold.
My billy goat, the boss man of my flock,
Had wandered away somewhere, away from the others.
Then I saw Daphnis and Daphnis caught sight of me
And he called out, "O Meliboeus, come here,
Come here and sit in the shade, and rest yourself.
Your goats and kids are perfectly safe and sound;
Your oxen will come this way all by themselves
Across the fields and down to the stream to drink
From Mincius' cool waters where the reeds
Flower along the riverbanks and where
The bees are humming around the ancient oak."
I thought, why not? I have no Phyllis at home
And no Alcippe to care for the just-weaned lambs,
But Corydon and Thyrsis in a contest
Is a contest not to miss.

The rural scene is very actual, the she-goats' udders brimming with milk, Meliboeus mulching his plants to protect them from the cold, no Phyllis or Alcippe at home to share his chores, his billy goat wandering off. The river Mincius is the actual river of Virgil's own childhood. Daphnis and Corydon and Thyrsis are local herdsmen and shepherds. But they have names from literature, from Theocritean Idylls, and two of them, Corydon and Thyrsis, who are like flowers in bloom, are not from Italy but from Arcadia, matrix of pastoral song. The verse that tells

us this is utterly unsurprised and unperturbed by the juxtaposition of fantasy to actuality, taking it for granted and thereby making each element, fantasy and actuality, and the oddness of their coming together, all the more vivid.

There was a Meliboeus in Eclogue I, dispossessed of his farm and going into exile, leading his poor little goats along with him:

> . . . one of them I could hardly get to follow;
> Just now, among the hazels, she went into labor
> And then, right there on the hard flinty ground,
> Gave birth to twins who would have been our hope,
> Back on our farm.

He is a different goatherd in Eclogue VII; or, if he is the same, then he has been given back his farm, or else has not yet been dispossessed of it—a magical restoration or the foreboding of a loss to come, and of course therefore both, restoration and loss, at once. There was a Daphnis in Eclogue V, who died and was apotheosized. This Daphnis, in Eclogue VII, may not be the same, since this is a different song, but because of the name the sense of a miraculous resuscitation is inescapable here, along with the sense that the death that has not yet taken place is surely coming. Daphnis is only a shepherd, but there is something god-like in his sweet hospitable authority here. We remember that when Daphnis was apotheosized in Eclogue V "the countryside, the woods . . . [were] all of them filled at once with holiday bliss," and this affects the way we hear this Daphnis, in Eclogue VII, say, as he invites Meliboeus to take a rest from his labor: "O Meliboeus, come here, / Come here and sit in the shade, and rest yourself. / Your goats and kids are perfectly safe and sound." It is all naturalistic; but there's something holy and magical about it too, because it is Daphnis speaking, as if he were the confident protector of the beasts and of the scene. The lines "Your oxen will come this way all by themselves / Across the fields and down to the stream to drink" remind us, too, of Eclogue IV and its prophecy that in the new Golden Age there will always be holiday joy and "The goats will come back home all by themselves / Without being called, their udders full of milk; / The browsing herds will have no fear of lions." The beasts in Eclogue VII will come down to drink from a stream "where the reeds /

Flower along the riverbanks and where / The bees are humming around the ancient oak." We remember that it was Meliboeus, dispossessed, who said to Tityrus, in Eclogue I, with unrancorous envy: "Often beside the hedge of willows that marks / This edge of what you own, the humming of bees / That visit the willow flowers will make you sleepy." The passage from Eclogue VII is sad as well as joyful, with the sadness that haunts the entire book. As Paul Alpers says, "Virgil's shepherds regularly come together for song and song is what unites them. But . . . separation and loss are the conditions of their utterance."[3] In this passage the shade, relief from labor and from the heat, engenders ease and music. But in Eclogue X, as the book of Eclogues itself comes to an end, the poet says, "Now we must go; the shade's not good for singers."

Wendell Clausen says that "pastoral, as a form of poetry (for pastoral moments occur in earlier Greek poetry), is the invention of Theocritus of Syracuse,"[4] and Paul Alpers says that pastoral "was, as the horsebreeders say, by Virgil out of Theocritus. Historically it was the work of both poets . . . It is from Virgil's self-conscious handling of Theocritean representations and usages that the figure of the herdsman emerged as representative both of the poet and of all humans."[5] There's nothing in those Idylls of Theocritus that corresponds to the way Virgil makes us aware of the world of politics, economics, and war, whose pressures are felt within and upon his pastoral world. Richard Tarrant has said that "the *Eclogues* are paradoxically both the work in which contemporary events are most pervasively present and the one in which they are most thoroughly transformed to subordinate them to a poetic context."[6]

And not just "contemporary events" but the range of things that human beings actually experience, long for, and lose are pervasively there in the Eclogues, and they are so in strangely beautiful and convincing ways because of their transformation and subordination to a poetic context. The Eclogues are a radical instance of what is always true of poetry: our vivid consciousness of the artifice of its forms makes us vividly, radiantly, conscious of our experience of its meanings. Of course this is always true in good poetry, but its truth with regard to the Eclogues has a special intense relationship to the pretense that it is shepherds talking, alone or together, and not just talking but singing, "song replying to song replying to song" (*et cantare pares et respondere parati*).

It is no wonder that the pastoral structure established in the book of Eclogues has, as resource and model, so deeply affected subsequent literature in all the languages of Europe. In these pastoral situations our faults and virtues are written large; the pastoral structure simplifies what we all share and, by doing so, makes it more tolerable while at the same time demonstrating how vulnerable we are. It provides figures of refuge and ease, and of the precariousness of that refuge and ease. It is associated with the essential, in its simplicity, and because the occupations of its actors, tilling the soil, tending the animals, are themselves essential and seem to go back to the beginning of time.

There were few immediate imitators of the Eclogues in Latin literature, but their influence in later centuries, in all the vernacular languages of Europe, has been powerful and, for good reason, has gone very deep. To speak only of literature in English, there are the works whose descent from the Eclogues is explicit—as in Spenser's *The Shepheardes Calender,* Sidney's "Ye Goatherd Gods," Marlowe's "Passionate Shepherd," Marvell's "Mower" poems, Milton's "Lycidas," Pope's "Pastorals," Book VIII of Wordsworth's *The Prelude,* Shelley's "Adonais," Matthew Arnold's "Thyrsis," Frost's "Build Soil"—or deeply implicit— as in passages of Shakespeare's *The Winter's Tale, The Tempest,* Marvell's "The Garden," Milton's *Paradise Lost,* Gray's "Elegy Written in a Country Churchyard," lyric after lyric of Wordsworth, the songs of Blake, Keats's "Ode to a Nightingale," lyric after lyric of Frost, and so much else. The Eclogues are everywhere.

Virgil's *Bucolica,* which we know as *The Eclogues,*[7] are his earliest authenticated work, dating at the latest from the mid-30s B.C.E. The next work, the four books of the *Georgics,* are said to have been read to Augustus in 29. Virgil began the writing of his epic of the founding of Rome, the *Aeneid,* shortly afterward and had almost completed it when, attempting to return to Rome after three years in Greece and Asia Minor, he fell ill, and died at Brundisium in September, 19 B.C.E. He was buried near Naples, where he owned a villa.

He had left orders that his unfinished *Aeneid* be burned, but Augustus ordered his literary executors Varius Rufus and Plotius Tucca to preserve it and publish it. It was issued two years later.

<div style="text-align:right">D.F.</div>

THE ECLOGUES

OF VIRGIL

ECLOGA I

[MELIBOEUS / TITYRUS]

MELIBOEUS

Tityre, tu patulae recubans sub tegmine fagi
siluestrem tenui Musam meditaris auena;
nos patriae finis et dulcia linquimus arua.
nos patriam fugimus; tu, Tityre, lentus in umbra
formosam resonare doces Amaryllida siluas.

TITYRUS

O Meliboee, deus nobis haec otia fecit.
namque erit ille mihi semper deus, illius aram
saepe tener nostris ab ouilibus imbuet agnus.
ille meas errare boues, ut cernis, et ipsum
ludere quae uellem calamo permisit agresti.

MELIBOEUS

Non equidem inuideo, miror magis: undique totis
usque adeo turbatur agris. en ipse capellas
protinus aeger ago; hanc etiam uix, Tityre, duco.
hic inter densas corylos modo namque gemellos,
spem gregis, a! silice in nuda conixa reliquit.
saepe malum hoc nobis, si mens non laeua fuisset,
de caelo tactas memini praedicere quercus.
sed tamen iste deus qui sit, da, Tityre, nobis.

ECLOGUE I

[MELIBOEUS / TITYRUS]

MELIBOEUS

Tityrus, there you lie in the beech-tree shade,
Brooding over your music for the Muse,
While we must leave our native place, our homes,
The fields we love, and go elsewhere; meanwhile,
You teach the woods to echo 'Amaryllis.'

TITYRUS

O Meliboeus, a god gave me this peace.
He will always be a god to me, and often
The blood of a newborn lamb will be offered to him.
Because of him, as you can see, my cattle
Can browse in the fields as they please, and as I please,
I idly play upon my slender reed.

MELIBOEUS

It's not that I'm envious, but full of wonder.
There's so much trouble everywhere these days.
I was trying to drive my goats along the path
And one of them I could hardly get to follow;
Just now, among the hazels, she went into labor
And then, right there on the hard flinty ground,
Gave birth to twins who would have been our hope,
Back on our farm. I should have been able to tell
That something like this was going to happen to us,

Vrbem quam dicunt Romam, Meliboee, putaui
stultus ego huic nostrae similem, quo saepe solemus
pastores ouium teneros depellere fetus.
sic canibus catulos similis, sic matribus haedos
noram, sic paruis componere magna solebam.
uerum haec tantum alias inter caput extulit urbes
quantum lenta solent inter uiburna cupressi.

MELIBOEUS

Et quae tanta fuit Romam tibi causa uidendi?

TITYRUS

Libertas, quae sera tamen respexit inertem,
candidior postquam tondenti barba cadebat,
respexit tamen et longo post tempore uenit,
postquam nos Amaryllis habet, Galatea reliquit.
namque (fatebor enim) dum me Galatea tenebat,
nec spes libertatis erat nec cura peculi.
quamuis multa meis exiret uictima saeptis,
pinguis et ingratae premeretur caseus urbi,
non umquam grauis aere domum mihi dextra redibat.

MELIBOEUS

Mirabar quid maesta deos, Amarylli, uocares,
cui pendere sua patereris in arbore poma;
Tityrus hinc aberat. ipsae te, Tityre, pinus,
ipsi te fontes, ipsa haec arbusta uocabant.

When the lightning struck our oak the other day.

But Tityrus, what god is this you speak of?

<center>TITYRUS</center>

I used to be silly enough to think the big
City of Rome was comparable to the town
To which we drive our tender lambs to market,
As grown-up dogs are comparable to puppies,
Or grown-up goats are comparable to kids,
But Rome is as much taller than other cities
As cypress trees than the little viburnums below them.

<center>MELIBOEUS</center>

How did it come about that you went to Rome?

<center>TITYRUS</center>

Well, freedom took her own sweet time about it
And waited till my first gray hairs showed up
In the haircut cuttings, but, however late,
She came along at last and favored me.
This was just at the time when Galatea
Left me and just at the time when I became
Possessed by Amaryllis. When I belonged
To Galatea I certainly had no hope
Of saving any money; I wasn't free.
Many a beast I took to town for slaughter,
And carried many a rich cheese there to sell,
And I can't say I ever brought home much
Money to show for what I'd brought to market.

<center>MELIBOEUS</center>

I wondered, Amaryllis, why you grieved so,
And called out to the gods, and why the apples
Were left to hang neglected in your orchards.
For Tityrus was gone; he wasn't there;
The pines called out for him, the springs, the orchards.

<center></center>

Quid facerem? neque seruitio me exire licebat
nec tam praesentis alibi cognoscere diuos.
hic illum uidi iuuenem, Meliboee, quotannis
bis senos cui nostra dies altaria fumant.
hic mihi responsum primus dedit ille petenti:
'pascite ut ante boues, pueri; summittite tauros.'

MELIBOEUS

Fortunate senex, ergo tua rura manebunt
et tibi magna satis, quamuis lapis omnia nudus
limosoque palus obducat pascua iunco:
non insueta grauis temptabunt pabula fetas,
nec mala uicini pecoris contagia laedent.
fortunate senex, hic inter flumina nota
et fontis sacros frigus captabis opacum;
hinc tibi, quae semper, uicino ab limite saepes
Hyblaeis apibus florem depasta salicti
saepe leui somnum suadebit inire susurro;
hinc alta sub rupe canet frondator ad auras,
nec tamen interea raucae, tua cura, palumbes
nec gemere aëria cessabit turtur ab ulmo.

TITYRUS

Ante leues ergo pascentur in aethere cerui
et freta destituent nudos in litore piscis,
ante pererratis amborum finibus exsul
aut Ararim Parthus bibet aut Germania Tigrim,
quam nostro illius labatur pectore uultus.

What else could I do? I couldn't otherwise
Be free of servitude, and I couldn't find
Gods anywhere else to help me out, but there
In Rome I found the young man in whose honor
We sacrifice at our altars every month.
He said, "Go feed your flocks as in the old days;
Herdsmen, raise your cattle as you used to."

MELIBOEUS

Most fortunate old man, no matter if
Your fields are stony or, by the brook's edge, marshy
And weedy, still they're yours, and enough for you.
No unaccustomed fodder there will tempt
Your pregnant ewes nor will your flock be threatened
By bad diseases from your neighbor's farm.
O fortunate Tityrus, lucky old man,
Here you will seek and find the cool of the shade
Beside your hallowed springs and the streams you know;
Often beside the hedge of willows that marks
This edge of what you own, the humming of bees
That visit the willow flowers will make you sleepy;
And over there, at the other edge of your land,
Under the ledge of that high outcropping of rock,
The song of a woodman pruning the trees can be heard;
And always you can hear your pigeons throating
And the moaning of the doves high in the elm tree.

TITYRUS

Stags will browse in the pastures of the air
And the sea will cast up its fish on the naked shore,
The exiled Parthian drink from the river Saône
And the German drink from the Tigris, before that face,
The way he looked at me, will fade from my heart.

At nos hinc alii sitientis ibimus Afros,
pars Scythiam et rapidum cretae ueniemus Oaxen
et penitus toto diuisos orbe Britannos.
en umquam patrios longo post tempore finis
pauperis et tuguri congestum caespite culmen,
post aliquot, mea regna, uidens mirabor aristas?
impius haec tam culta noualia miles habebit,
barbarus has segetes. en quo discordia ciuis
produxit miseros: his nos conseuimus agros!
insere nunc, Meliboee, piros, pone ordine uitis.
ite meae, felix quondam pecus, ite capellae.
non ego uos posthac uiridi proiectus in antro
dumosa pendere procul de rupe uidebo;
carmina nulla canam; non me pascente, capellae,
florentem cytisum et salices carpetis amaras.

Hic tamen hanc mecum poteras requiescere noctem
fronde super uiridi: sunt nobis mitia poma,
castaneae molles et pressi copia lactis,
et iam summa procul uillarum culmina fumant
maioresque cadunt altis de montibus umbrae.

But *we* have to leave our homes and go far away,
Some to the thirsty deserts of Africa,
Some to Scythia, some to the region where
Oaxes rushes over its chalky bed,
Some as far away as among the Britons,
Utterly cut off from all the world.
Oh, will it ever come to pass that I'll
Come back, after many years, to look upon
The turf roof of what had been my cottage
And the little field of grain that once was mine,
My own little kingdom. Have we done all this work
Upon our planted and fallow fields so that
Some godless barbarous soldier will enjoy it?
This is what civil war has brought down upon us.
So Meliboeus, carefully set out
Your plants and pear trees, all in rows—for whom?
For strangers, for others, we have farmed our land.

Come on, my goats, once happy flock, go on.
Never again will I, stretched out at ease
In the mouth of some mossy cave, see how, far off,
Browsing you seem to hang from the high cliff side;
No longer will I sing my songs; no more,
My goats, will I watch over you as you crop
The flowering clover and the acrid willow.

Nevertheless, tonight you might stay here
And rest yourself awhile on these green fronds;
The apples are ripe, the chestnuts are plump and mealy,
There's plenty of good pressed cheese you're welcome to.
Already there's smoke you can see from the neighbors' chimneys
And the shadows of the hills are lengthening as they fall.

ECLOGA II

Formosum pastor Corydon ardebat Alexin,
delicias domini, nec quid speraret habebat.
tantum inter densas, umbrosa cacumina, fagos
adsidue ueniebat. ibi haec incondita solus
montibus et siluis studio iactabat inani:
 'O crudelis Alexi, nihil mea carmina curas?
nil nostri miserere? mori me denique cogis?
nunc etiam pecudes umbras et frigora captant,
nunc uiridis etiam occultant spineta lacertos,
Thestylis et rapido fessis messoribus aestu
alia serpyllumque herbas contundit olentis.
at mecum raucis, tua dum uestigia lustro,
sole sub ardenti resonant arbusta cicadis.
nonne fuit satius tristis Amaryllidis iras
atque superba pati fastidia? nonne Menalcan,
quamuis ille niger, quamuis tu candidus esses?
o formose puer, nimium ne crede colori:
alba ligustra cadunt, uaccinia nigra leguntur.
despectus tibi sum, nec qui sim quaeris, Alexi,
quam diues pecoris, niuei quam lactis abundans.

ECLOGUE II

[VIRGIL / CORYDON]

Corydon fell in love with a beautiful boy
Whose name was Alexis, the darling of his master.
So every day of the week he took himself
To the dense and gloomy shade of a beech-tree grove,
And flung out his hopeless ardor in artless verses:

"O cruel Alexis, why are you deaf to my songs?
Have you no pity at all? Or don't you know
That Corydon's going to die for love of you?
Even the cows are seeking out the shade,
The little green lizards are hiding themselves in the bushes,
The laborers are worn out from the heat,
And Thestylis is pounding garlic and thyme,
Getting lunch ready, but under the burning sun
There's only my voice and the voice of the wailing locust.
Oh, wouldn't I have done better to put up with
The anger and haughty disdain of Amaryllis?
Or with Menalcas, swarthy though he is?
O fair Alexis, don't put too much trust
In your complexion. Remember that the blossoms
Of white privet fade and the darker blossoms
Of hyacinths are what the gatherers gather.
Perhaps you do not know, Alexis, who
It is you scorn: how many cows I have,
With all the milk they yield, summer and winter;

mille meae Siculis errant in montibus agnae;
lac mihi non aestate nouum, non frigore defit.
canto quae solitus, si quando armenta uocabat,
Amphion Dircaeus in Actaeo Aracyntho.
nec sum adeo informis: nuper me in litore uidi,
cum placidum uentis staret mare. non ego Daphnin
iudice te metuam, si numquam fallit imago.
o tantum libeat mecum tibi sordida rura
atque humilis habitare casas et figere ceruos,
haedorumque gregem uiridi compellere hibisco!
mecum una in siluis imitabere Pana canendo
(Pan primum calamos cera coniungere pluris
instituit, Pan curat ouis ouiumque magistros),
nec te paeniteat calamo triuisse labellum:
haec eadem ut sciret, quid non faciebat Amyntas?
est mihi disparibus septem compacta cicutis
fistula, Damoetas dono mihi quam dedit olim,
et dixit moriens: 'te nunc habet ista secundum';
dixit Damoetas, inuidit stultus Amyntas.
praeterea duo nec tuta mihi ualle reperti
capreoli, sparsis etiam nunc pellibus albo,
bina die siccant ouis ubera; quos tibi seruo.
iam pridem a me illos abducere Thestylis orat;
et faciet, quoniam sordent tibi munera nostra.
huc ades, o formose puer: tibi lilia plenis
ecce ferunt Nymphae calathis; tibi candida Nais,
pallentis uiolas et summa papauera carpens,
narcissum et florem iungit bene olentis anethi;

A thousand lambs, my lambs, pasture upon
These hills around; my voice is like the voice
Of Amphion on the slopes of Aracynthus,
Calling his herds. Nor is it that I'm bad-looking.
The other day when the wind was entirely still
And the sea was therefore like a mirror I saw
Myself in the mirror and said to myself that I,
If mirrors tell the truth, you being the judge,
Need never fear comparison with Daphnis.

"O come and live with me in the countryside,
Among the humble farms. Together we
Will hunt the deer, and tend the little goats,
Compelling them along with willow wands.
Together singing we will mimic Pan,
Who was the first who taught how reeds could be
Bound together with wax to make a pipe.
Pan takes care of the shepherd and the sheep.
You oughtn't to mind if the reed bruises your lip;
Think how Amyntas practiced, learning to play.
Damoetas when he was dying bequeathed to me
This pipe I have, of seven hemlock stalks
Of different lengths. 'Now you're its master,' he said,
And foolish Amyntas was full of envy of me.
Besides the pipe I have two fawns I found
In a dangerous nearby valley, still so young
Their coats are speckled with white and eagerly
They feed at the udder of one of my ewes as if
They were really baby lambs; I've saved them for you;
Thestylis keeps telling me she wants them,
And maybe I'll give them to her, since it is clear
How little you think of the gifts I offer you.
O beautiful Alexis, come, see how
The Nymphs are bringing you baskets full of lilies,
See, the lovely Naiad makes a bouquet
Of palest violets and scarlet poppies for you,
Flower of fennel, narcissus blossoms also,

tum casia atque aliis intexens suauibus herbis
mollia luteola pingit uaccinia calta.
ipse ego cana legam tenera lanugine mala
castaneasque nuces, mea quas Amaryllis amabat;
addam cerea pruna (honos erit huic quoque pomo),
et uos, o lauri, carpam et te, proxima myrte,
sic positae quoniam suauis miscetis odores.
rusticus es, Corydon; nec munera curat Alexis,
nec, si muneribus certes, concedat Iollas.
heu heu, quid uolui misero mihi? floribus Austrum
perditus et liquidis immisi fontibus apros.
quem fugis, a! demens? habitarunt di quoque siluas
Dardaniusque Paris. Pallas quas condidit arces
ipsa colat; nobis placeant ante omnia siluae.
torua leaena lupum sequitur, lupus ipse capellam,
florentem cytisum sequitur lasciua capella,
te Corydon, o Alexi: trahit sua quemque uoluptas.
aspice, aratra iugo referunt suspensa iuuenci,
et sol crescentis decedens duplicat umbras;
me tamen urit amor: quis enim modus adsit amori?
a, Corydon, Corydon, quae te dementia cepit!
semiputata tibi frondosa uitis in ulmo est:
quin tu aliquid saltem potius, quorum indiget usus,
uiminibus mollique paras detexere iunco?
inuenies alium, si te hic fastidit, Alexin.'

With yellow marigold and hyacinth,
And bound together with twine of cassia
And other fragrant herbs. And I myself
Will gather chestnuts as an offering,
And also downy peaches, and waxen plums,
Such as my Amaryllis used to love;
And I'll pluck laurel too, and the nearby myrtle,
The mingled perfume of them being so sweet.

"Corydon, you're a yokel. What makes you think
Alexis would care in the least about what you offer?
And as for gifts, would Iollas offer less?
Alas, alas, what have unhappy I
Been hoping for? In my distraction I
Have brought the sirocco down upon my flowers
And let the wild boar in to my crystal springs.
Ah, whom are you fleeing? A madman! Even the gods
Have lived in the woods, and Paris lived there too.
Let Pallas live in the city that she founded.
Let me dwell here lamenting in the forest.
The fierce lioness follows after the wolf,
The wolf pursues the goat, the wanton goat
Seeks out the flowering clover in the field,
And Corydon, Alexis, follows you.
Each creature is led by that which it most longs for.

"Look, here are the oxen come in from the fields,
Dragging the plow behind them, as the sun
Causes the shadows to lengthen and multiply,
And I still burn with love; love knows no limits.
Ah, Corydon, what madness has hold of you?
The vine on the leafy elm is only half-pruned—
Why not at least go about some needful task,
Binding the twigs together with pliant rushes.
There'll be another Alexis, if this one rejects you."

ECLOGA III

[MENALCAS / DAMOETAS / PALAEMON]

MENALCAS
Dic mihi, Damoeta, cuium pecus? an Meliboei?

DAMOETAS
Non, uerum Aegonis; nuper mihi tradidit Aegon.

MENALCAS
Infelix o semper, oues, pecus! ipse Neaeram
dum fouet ac ne me sibi praeferat illa ueretur,
hic alienus ouis custos bis mulget in hora,
et sucus pecori et lac subducitur agnis.

DAMOETAS
Parcius ista uiris tamen obicienda memento.
nouimus et qui te transuersa tuentibus hircis
et quo (sed faciles Nymphae risere) sacello.

MENALCAS
Tum, credo, cum me arbustum uidere Miconis
atque mala uitis incidere falce nouellas.

ECLOGUE III

[MENALCAS / DAMOETAS / PALAEMON]

MENALCAS

Whose flock is this? Is it Meliboeus's flock?

DAMOETAS

No, it's Aegon's flock. He put me in charge of it.

MENALCAS

O you poor sheep, you poor unlucky sheep.
While Aegon's somewhere trying to make Neaera,
Hoping she doesn't like me better than him,
He puts somebody ignorant like you
In charge of his flock. You'll probably milk the ewes
Every half hour and dry up their strength and so
The little lambs won't have any milk to grow on.

DAMOETAS

Watch out what you say, Menalcas, because I know
What you were doing in that cave and who
You were doing it with, while the goats looked on,
Rolling their eyes, and the laughing Nymphs were watching.

MENALCAS

That was the day, no doubt, when it was *me*
Who got caught with a knife cutting down Micon's
New little vines purely out of spite?

Aut hic ad ueteres fagos cum Daphnidis arcum
fregisti et calamos: quae tu, peruerse Menalca,
et cum uidisti puero donata, dolebas,
et si non aliqua nocuisses, mortuus esses.

MENALCAS

Quid domini faciant, audent cum talia fures?
non ego te uidi Damonis, pessime, caprum
excipere insidiis multum latrante Lycisca?
et cum clamarem 'quo nunc se proripit ille?
Tityre, coge pecus', tu post carecta latebas.

DAMOETAS

An mihi cantando uictus non redderet ille,
quem mea carminibus meruisset fistula caprum?
si nescis, meus ille caper fuit; et mihi Damon
ipse fatebatur, sed reddere posse negabat.

MENALCAS

Cantando tu illum? aut umquam tibi fistula cera
iuncta fuit? non tu in triuiis, indocte, solebas
stridenti miserum stipula disperdere carmen?

DAMOETAS

Vis ergo inter nos quid possit uterque uicissim
experiamur? ego hanc uitulam (ne forte recuses,
bis uenit ad mulctram, binos alit ubere fetus)
depono; tu dic mecum quo pignore certes.

MENALCAS

De grege non ausim quicquam deponere tecum:
est mihi namque domi pater, est iniusta nouerca,

Maybe it was the day, right here, near these beeches,
When you broke Daphnis' bow and his arrows too,
Because you couldn't stand the idea, you prick,
That that boy was given them as a song-prize.
You were dying to get back at him.

MENALCAS

 I saw you
Trying to steal a goat from Damon's flock
While Damon's dog was barking and I was hollering,
"Look what's happening! Where's he running to?
Tityrus, round up the flock!" And there you were,
Crouching behind the hedge.

DAMOETAS

 I won that goat
With my flute and my singing at the singing contest.
It was my goat. I won it. And Damon knew it.
And he didn't pay up.

MENALCAS

 You beat *him*? Damon? At singing?
When did you expect you'd ever have
A proper flute to play? Aren't you the one
Who used to murder some song, down by the crossroads,
Screeching away through a whining pipe of straw?

DAMOETAS

You want to take turns and see which one is best?
I'll put up this cow. She has two calves and still
Twice every day she comes to the milking-stool.
So what will you put up?

MENALCAS

 No animals.
My father and my mean stepmother take turns

bisque die numerant ambo pecus, alter et haedos.
uerum, id quod multo tute ipse fatebere maius
(insanire libet quoniam tibi), pocula ponam
fagina, caelatum diuini opus Alcimedontis,
lenta quibus torno facili superaddita uitis
diffusos hedera uestit pallente corymbos.
in medio duo signa, Conon et—quis fuit alter,
descripsit radio totum qui gentibus orbem,
tempora quae messor, quae curuus arator haberet?
necdum illis labra admoui, sed condita seruo.

DAMOETAS

Et nobis idem Alcimedon duo pocula fecit
et molli circum est ansas amplexus acantho,
Orpheaque in medio posuit siluasque sequentis;
necdum illis labra admoui, sed condita seruo.
si ad uitulam spectas, nihil est quod pocula laudes.

MENALCAS

Numquam hodie effugies; ueniam quocumque uocaris.
audiat haec tantum—uel qui uenit ecce Palaemon.
efficiam posthac ne quemquam uoce lacessas.

DAMOETAS

Quin age, si quid habes; in me mora non erit ulla,
nec quemquam fugio: tantum, uicine Palaemon,
sensibus haec imis (res est non parua) reponas.

PALAEMON

Dicite, quandoquidem in molli consedimus herba.
et nunc omnis ager, nunc omnis parturit arbos,

Counting the flock, twice a day without fail,
Including the kids. But since you're dumb enough
To bet on yourself, you're going to have to admit
What I'll put up is better. I'm putting up
Two cups made out of beechwood and decorated
By Alcimedon, the best at things like this.
They've got a spreading vine engraved on them,
Entangled with pale clusters of ivy and
Two human figures in the middle, one
Is Conon and the other—what was his name?—
The one who portioned out the range of the sky
And showed what time was best for the reaper's work
And what time best for the bent-backed plowman's work?
I've stored these cups; my lips have never touched them.

DAMOETAS

Well, Alcimedon made two cups for me,
He twined acanthus around the handles and pictured
Orpheus in the middle, followed by trees.
I've stored these cups; my lips have never touched them.
But when you see my cow you won't praise cups.

MENALCAS

Don't think you'll get away from me today.
I'll meet you any time and place you say.
Who'll be the witness?—Look, here comes Palaemon!
I'll see to it that after this you'll challenge
Nobody ever again.

DAMOETAS
 Put up or shut up. Now,
Let's go, I'm ready. But, neighbor Palaemon, please
Pay close attention. This is serious business.

PALAEMON

Now we are seated here on the soft grass,
Begin the singing. The fields have begun to flower;

nunc frondent siluae, nunc formosissimus annus.
incipe, Damoeta; tu deinde sequere, Menalca.
alternis dicetis; amant alterna Camenae.

DAMOETAS

Ab Ioue principium Musae: Iouis omnia plena;
ille colit terras, illi mea carmina curae.

MENALCAS

Et me Phoebus amat; Phoebo sua semper apud me
munera sunt, lauri et suaue rubens hyacinthus.

DAMOETAS

Malo me Galatea petit, lasciua puella,
et fugit ad salices et se cupit ante uideri.

MENALCAS

At mihi sese offert ultro, meus ignis, Amyntas,
notior ut iam sit canibus non Delia nostris.

DAMOETAS

Parta meae Veneri sunt munera: namque notaui
ipse locum, aëriae quo congessere palumbes.

MENALCAS

Quod potui, puero siluestri ex arbore lecta
aurea mala decem misi; cras altera mittam.

DAMOETAS

O quotiens et quae nobis Galatea locuta est!
partem aliquam, uenti, diuum referatis ad auris!

MENALCAS

Quid prodest quod me ipse animo non spernis, Amynta,
si, dum tu sectaris apros, ego retia seruo?

The trees are budding and the woods are green;
The year is at its nicest moment now.
Begin, Damoetas, sing, and then, Menalcas;
You each shall sing in turn, so please the Muses.

DAMOETAS

"Muses, my song begins in praise of Jove;
He makes all flourish; my song is in his care."

MENALCAS

"Apollo loves me. Together we gather laurel
And the blushing hyacinth, his favorite."

DAMOETAS

"Fair Galatea pelts me with apples and runs
To hide in the woods and wishes to be found."

MENALCAS

"Amyntas comes to me of his own accord;
Delia's not better known to our household dogs."

DAMOETAS

"I've found the gifts to bring to my Galatea;
I know where the wood doves nest high up in the branches."

MENALCAS

"I sent him ten gold apples from a tree,
All I could find; tomorrow I'll send ten more."

DAMOETAS

"Let the breezes tell to the gods only a part
Of what my Galatea said to me."

MENALCAS

"What good does it do, Amyntas, that you love me,
If I have to mind the nets while you go hunting."

DAMOETAS

Phyllida mitte mihi: meus est natalis, Iolla;
cum faciam uitula pro frugibus, ipse uenito.

MENALCAS

Phyllida amo ante alias; nam me discedere fleuit
et longum 'formose, uale, uale,' inquit, 'Iolla.'

DAMOETAS

Triste lupus stabulis, maturis frugibus imbres,
arboribus uenti, nobis Amaryllidis irae.

MENALCAS

Dulce satis umor, depulsis arbutus haedis,
lenta salix feto pecori, mihi solus Amyntas.

DAMOETAS

Pollio amat nostram, quamuis est rustica, Musam:
Pierides, uitulam lectori pascite uestro.

MENALCAS

Pollio et ipse facit noua carmina: pascite taurum,
iam cornu petat et pedibus qui spargat harenam.

DAMOETAS

Qui te, Pollio, amat, ueniat quo te quoque gaudet;
mella fluant illi, ferat et rubus asper amomum.

MENALCAS

Qui Bauium non odit, amet tua carmina, Maeui,
atque idem iungat uulpes et mulgeat hircos.

DAMOETAS

Qui legitis flores et humi nascentia fraga,
frigidus, o pueri (fugite hinc!), latet anguis in herba.

DAMOETAS

"Send Phyllis here, Iollas, it's my birthday;
You come when the calf is sacrificed for the fields."

MENALCAS

"I love Phyllis best because when I left her she wept
And sadly said, 'Farewell, farewell, fair Iollas.'"

DAMOETAS

"The anger of Amaryllis is to me
As the wolf to the flock, the wind to the vines and crops."

MENALCAS

"As rain to the corn, arbutus to weanling kids,
Willows to breeding cows, Amyntas to me."

DAMOETAS

"Pollio loves my songs, however clumsy;
Muses, offer a calf to placate readers."

MENALCAS

"And Pollio too writes songs; offer a bull
With butting horns, and hooves that paw the ground."

DAMOETAS

"May Pollio's lovers be where Pollio is:
Where the honey flows, and the spicebush flourishes."

MENALCAS

"May Bavius' lovers admire Mevius' verses,
Milk billy goats, yoke foxes to their plows."

DAMOETAS

"You boys gathering flowers and picking strawberries,
Watch out, watch out, there's a cold snake in the grass."

.

Parcite, oues, nimium procedere: non bene ripae
creditur; ipse aries etiam nunc uellera siccat.

DAMOETAS

Tityre, pascentis a flumine reice capellas:
ipse, ubi tempus erit, omnis in fonte lauabo.

MENALCAS

Cogite ouis, pueri: si lac praeceperit aestus,
ut nuper, frustra pressabimus ubera palmis.

DAMOETAS

Heu heu, quam pingui macer est mihi taurus in eruo!
idem amor exitium pecori pecorisque magistro.

MENALCAS

His certe neque amor causa est; uix ossibus haerent;
nescio quis teneros oculus mihi fascinat agnos.

DAMOETAS

Dic quibus in terris (et eris mihi magnus Apollo)
tris pateat caeli spatium non amplius ulnas.

MENALCAS

Dic quibus in terris inscripti nomina regum
nascantur flores, et Phyllida solus habeto.

PALAEMON

Non nostrum inter uos tantas componere lites:
et uitula tu dignus et hic, et quisquis amores
aut metuet dulcis aut experietur amaros.
claudite iam riuos, pueri; sat prata biberunt.

"Don't go too near the riverbank, my sheep;
The river's high; the ram has gotten wet."

DAMOETAS

"Tityrus, keep the goats away from the river;
I'll wash them in the pond when it's time to wash them."

MENALCAS

"Round up the sheep, boys, find the cool of the shade;
This heat will dry the milk up in the udders."

DAMOETAS

"My bull is thin although there's plenty to browse on;
Love is the trouble both for the bull and his master."

MENALCAS

"My flock is skin and bones, and it isn't for love;
The evil eye is on my lambs. But whose?"

DAMOETAS

"You'll be Apollo if you can tell me where
The land is, where the sky is five feet wide."

MENALCAS

"Phyllis is yours if you can tell me where
The flowers bloom with royal names inscribed."

PALAEMON

I don't know how to arbitrate this great
Debate between you two. You both deserve
To win the prize, and so do all who have
Experienced the sweet and bitter of love.
But the time has come to close the sluices, boys,
For now the fields have drunk their fill of song.

ECLOGA IV

Sicelides Musae, paulo maiora canamus!
non omnis arbusta iuuant humilesque myricae;
si canimus siluas, siluae sint consule dignae.
 Ultima Cumaei uenit iam carminis aetas;
magnus ab integro saeclorum nascitur ordo.
iam redit et Virgo, redeunt Saturnia regna,
iam noua progenies caelo demittitur alto.
tu modo nascenti puero, quo ferrea primum
desinet ac toto surget gens aurea mundo,
casta faue Lucina: tuus iam regnat Apollo.
teque adeo decus hoc aeui, te consule, inibit,
Pollio, et incipient magni procedere menses;
te duce, si qua manent sceleris uestigia nostri,
inrita perpetua soluent formidine terras.
ille deum uitam accipiet diuisque uidebit
permixtos heroas et ipse uidebitur illis,
pacatumque reget patriis uirtutibus orbem.
 At tibi prima, puer, nullo munuscula cultu
errantis hederas passim cum baccare tellus

ECLOGUE IV

[VIRGIL]

Sicilian Muses, sing a nobler music,
For orchard trees and humble tamarisks
Do not please everyone; so may your song
Be of a forest worthy of a consul.
The last great age the Sybil told has come;
The new order of centuries is born;
The Virgin now returns, and the reign of Saturn;
The new generation now comes down from heaven.
Lucina, look with favor on this child,
—Lucina, goddess, pure—this child by whom
The Age of Iron gives way to the Golden Age.
Now is the time of your Apollo's reign;
And, Pollio, in your consulship, begins
The grand procession of the mighty months,
Commencement of the glory, freedom from
Earth's bondage to its own perpetual fear.
Our crimes are going to be erased at last.
This child will share in the life of the gods and he
Will see and be seen in the company of heroes,
And he will be the ruler of a world
Made peaceful by the merits of his father.

Dear child, there will be new little gifts for you,
Springtime valerian, and trailing ivy,

mixtaque ridenti colocasia fundet acantho.
ipsae lacte domum referent distenta capellae
ubera, nec magnos metuent armenta leones;
ipsa tibi blandos fundent cunabula flores.
occidet et serpens, et fallax herba ueneni
occidet; Assyrium uulgo nascetur amomum.
at simul heroum laudes et facta parentis
iam legere et quae sit poteris cognoscere uirtus,
molli paulatim flauescet campus arista
incultisque rubens pendebit sentibus uua
et durae quercus sudabunt roscida mella.
pauca tamen suberunt priscae uestigia fraudis,
quae temptare Thetim ratibus, quae cingere muris
oppida, quae iubeant telluri infindere sulcos.
alter erit tum Tiphys et altera quae uehat Argo
delectos heroas; erunt etiam altera bella
atque iterum ad Troiam magnus mittetur Achilles.
hinc, ubi iam firmata uirum te fecerit aetas,
cedet et ipse mari uector, nec nautica pinus
mutabit merces; omnis feret omnia tellus.
non rastros patietur humus, non uinea falcem;
robustus quoque iam tauris iuga soluet arator.
nec uarios discet mentiri lana colores,
ipse sed in pratis aries iam suaue rubenti
murice, iam croceo mutabit uellera luto;
sponte sua sandyx pascentis uestiet agnos.

Egyptian beans, and smiling acanthus, all
Poured out profusely from the untilled earth.
The goats will come back home all by themselves
Without being called, their udders full of milk;
The browsing herds will have no fear of lions;
Your cradle will be a cornucopia
Of smiling flowers blossoming around you;
Nowhere will there be serpents anymore,
And nowhere plants in which a poison hides;
And everywhere the Assyrian spice will flourish.

As soon as you are old enough to read
The praise of heroes and your father's deeds
And therefore know what excellence consists of,
The grain will yellow and ripen in the fields,
The purple grapes will cluster on wild vines,
And honey will drip like dew from the hard oak tree.
But there will still be vestiges of sin,
And therefore men will still be forced to try
The sea in ships, build walls around their towns,
And labor in their fields to plow their soil.
There will be need for yet another Argo
To carry its chosen heroes on their mission;
There'll be another war, and once again
Another Achilles will be called to Troy.
But when the years have brought your strength to manhood,
No longer then will merchant ships set forth
Laden with things to trade in foreign places;
Each land will bear of itself what it needs for itself;
The earth will suffer the harrow's tooth no longer
Nor vines suffer the claw of the pruning-hook;
No longer need cloth learn to imitate colors;
Out in the meadow the fleece of the ram will change
Of its own accord from purple to saffron yellow;
In the meadow the lambs will graze in bright red coats.

'Talia saecla' suis dixerunt 'currite' fusis
concordes stabili fatorum numine Parcae.
adgredere o magnos (aderit iam tempus) honores,
cara deum suboles, magnum Iouis incrementum!
aspice conuexo nutantem pondere mundum,
terrasque tractusque maris caelumque profundum;
aspice, uenturo laetentur ut omnia saeclo!
o mihi tum longae maneat pars ultima uitae,
spiritus et quantum sat erit tua dicere facta!
non me carminibus uincet nec Thracius Orpheus
nec Linus, huic mater quamuis atque huic pater adsit,
Orphei Calliopea, Lino formosus Apollo.
Pan etiam, Arcadia mecum si iudice certet,
Pan etiam Arcadia dicat se iudice uictum.

Incipe, parue puer, risu cognoscere matrem
(matri longa decem tulerunt fastidia menses)
incipe, parue puer: qui non risere parenti,
nec deus hunc mensa, dea nec dignata cubili est.

"So let all ages be like this," the Parcae,
Voicing the gods' unchangeable decree,
Cry out in unison to their whirling spindles.

O you dear child of the gods, increase of Jove,
The time has come about at last for you
To take upon you those great honors foretold;
Behold how the vaulted universe trembles in awe—
Earth and the range of sea and the depth of sky—
Glorying in the new age coming in.
Oh, if I have long life and at the end
Have breath enough and spirit enough to be
The teller of the story of your deeds,
Then neither Linus nor Thracian Orpheus could
Defeat me in the singing contest, though
Orpheus' mother, Calliope, were there,
And Linus' father, Apollo the beautiful;
And Pan himself, Arcadia the judge,
Judged by Arcadia, would admit defeat.
So, little baby, may your first smile be
When you first recognize your mother, whose
Long nine-months travail brought you into the world.
That child who has not smiled thus for his parents
No gods will welcome at their festive table
Nor any goddess to her amorous bower.

ECLOGA V

[MENALCAS / MOPSUS]

MENALCAS
Cur non, Mopse, boni quoniam conuenimus ambo,
tu calamos inflare leuis, ego dicere uersus,
hic corylis mixtas inter consedimus ulmos?

MOPSUS
Tu maior; tibi me est aequum parere, Menalca,
siue sub incertas Zephyris motantibus umbras
siue antro potius succedimus. aspice, ut antrum
siluestris raris sparsit labrusca racemis.

MENALCAS
Montibus in nostris solus tibi certat Amyntas.

MOPSUS
Quid, si idem certet Phoebum superare canendo?

MENALCAS
Incipe, Mopse, prior, si quos aut Phyllidis ignis
aut Alconis habes laudes aut iurgia Codri.
incipe: pascentis seruabit Tityrus haedos.

ECLOGUE V

[MENALCAS / MOPSUS]

MENALCAS

Mopsus, let us sit down together here
In this elm and hazel grove, two good musicians,
You at the shepherd's pipe and I at singing.

MOPSUS

You are the elder of us two, Menalcas,
Therefore you should choose where we should be,
Whether beneath these trees, within the shadows
That change and move as the breezes move and change them,
Or else within this cave that's near at hand—
See how the vine has spread its tendrils round
The entrance to the cave, with clustering flowers.

MENALCAS

You have no mountain rival but Amyntas.

MOPSUS

Do you think he wants to rival Apollo too?

MENALCAS

If you have one ready, Mopsus, play a song
In praise of Phyllis your love, or in praise of Alcon,
Or maybe play in fun one praising Codrus.
Tityrus will watch the grazing flock.

Immo haec, in uiridi nuper quae cortice fagi
carmina descripsi et modulans alterna notaui,
experiar: tu deinde iubeto ut certet Amyntas.

Lenta salix quantum pallenti cedit oliuae,
puniceis humilis quantum saliunca rosetis,
iudicio nostro tantum tibi cedit Amyntas.
sed tu desine plura, puer: successimus antro.

Exstinctum Nymphae crudeli funere Daphnin
flebant (uos coryli testes et flumina Nymphis),
cum complexa sui corpus miserabile nati
atque deos atque astra uocat crudelia mater.
non ulli pastos illis egere diebus
frigida, Daphni, boues ad flumina; nulla neque amnem
libauit quadripes nec graminis attigit herbam.
Daphni, tuum Poenos etiam ingemuisse leones
interitum montesque feri siluaeque loquuntur.
Daphnis et Armenias curru subiungere tigris
instituit, Daphnis thiasos inducere Bacchi
et foliis lentas intexere mollibus hastas.
uitis ut arboribus decori est, ut uitibus uuae,
ut gregibus tauri, segetes ut pinguibus aruis,
tu decus omne tuis. postquam te fata tulerunt,
ipsa Pales agros atque ipse reliquit Apollo.

I think, instead, I'll try these verses I carved
On a green beech tree the other afternoon.
First I marked out the words and then marked out
The music that I wrote to go with the words.
See if Amyntas can do as well as this.

MENALCAS

It seems to me Amyntas yields to you
As the willow bows to the pale green olive tree,
And the low wild nard gives precedence to the rose.

But now we are in the cavern. Begin your song.

MOPSUS

"The hazels and the rivers testify
How the Nymphs shed tears for Daphnis, as his mother,
Embracing the wretched body of her child,
So cruelly dead, cried out against the gods
And against the stars. In the days of this event
Nobody drove his cattle down to the brooks
To drink the cooling waters; no beast would drink;
And, Daphnis, the woods, the wilderness mountains told us
How, far away in Africa, the lions
Mourning in the desert could be heard.
It was Daphnis who yoked together the tigers to draw
The chariot of Bacchus, and it was Daphnis
Who led the Bacchic dance, and Daphnis who bound
The vine leaves and the fennel stalk together
To make the thyrsus of Bacchus. Just as the vine
Is the glory of the tree trunk that it clings to,
Just as the grape is the glory of its vine,
Just as the bull is the glory of its herd,
And the flourishing corn of the soil it grows from, Daphnis,
You are the glory of all the rest of us.
Now that the Fates have taken you away,
Apollo has left our fields, and Pales too.

grandia saepe quibus mandauimus hordea sulcis,
infelix lolium et steriles nascuntur auenae;
pro molli uiola, pro purpureo narcisso
carduus et spinis surgit paliurus acutis.
spargite humum foliis, inducite fontibus umbras,
pastores (mandat fieri sibi talia Daphnis),
et tumulum facite, et tumulo superaddite carmen:
'Daphnis ego in siluis, hinc usque ad sidera notus,
formosi pecoris custos, formosior ipse.'

MENALCAS

Tale tuum carmen nobis, diuine poeta,
quale sopor fessis in gramine, quale per aestum
dulcis aquae saliente sitim restinguere riuo.
nec calamis solum aequiperas, sed uoce magistrum:
fortunate puer, tu nunc eris alter ab illo.
nos tamen haec quocumque modo tibi nostra uicissim
dicemus, Daphninque tuum tollemus ad astra;
Daphnin ad astra feremus: amauit nos quoque Daphnis.

MOPSUS

An quicquam nobis tali sit munere maius?
et puer ipse fuit cantari dignus, et ista
iam pridem Stimichon laudauit carmina nobis.

MENALCAS

Candidus insuetum miratur limen Olympi
sub pedibusque uidet nubes et sidera Daphnis.
ergo alacris siluas et cetera rura uoluptas
Panaque pastoresque tenet Dryadasque puellas.
nec lupus insidias pecori, nec retia ceruis
ulla dolum meditantur: amat bonus otia Daphnis.
ipsi laetitia uoces ad sidera iactant
intonsi montes; ipsae iam carmina rupes,

In the furrows where we hopefully planted barley,
Darnel and tares and sterile oat-grass grow;
Where the violet and purple narcissus were,
Now thistle flourishes and spiky thorn.
Scatter the ground with flowers, all you shepherds,
And shade with mourning trees the woodland springs—
Thus Daphnis has commanded for his honor.
Then build a tomb and place on the tomb these verses:
'Daphnis was known to these woods and known to the stars;
Lovely the flock, and lovelier still the shepherd.'"

MENALCAS

Inspired poet, the song you sing is such
As sleep must be to the weary on the grass
Or cool brook water quenching the thirst of summer.
First after him you are, now, fortunate boy,
In singing as in playing worthy your master.
I nevertheless will sing as best I can,
Taking my turn, to raise your Daphnis up
Among the stars; Daphnis shall be high
Among the stars; I too was loved by Daphnis.

MOPSUS

Nothing could be a greater gift than this;
The boy himself was worthy of your song;
Stimichon long since has praised your singing.

MENALCAS

"Radiant Daphnis wonders at heaven's threshold,
Seeing the stars and clouds beneath his feet,
And therefore all the countryside, the woods,
And Pan, the Dryads, and the shepherds too,
Are all of them filled at once with holiday bliss;
No wolf lies down in ambush for the sheep,
No traps are set for the deer. Daphnis loves peace.
The unshorn mountains joyfully shout to the stars,
The groves and rocky places sing together,

ipsa sonant arbusta: 'deus, deus ille, Menalca!'
sis bonus o felixque tuis! en quattuor aras:
ecce duas tibi, Daphni, duas altaria Phoebo.
pocula bina nouo spumantia lacte quotannis
craterasque duo statuam tibi pinguis oliui,
et multo in primis hilarans conuiuia Baccho
(ante focum, si frigus erit; si messis, in umbra)
uina nouum fundam calathis Ariusia nectar.
cantabunt mihi Damoetas et Lyctius Aegon;
saltantis Satyros imitabitur Alphesiboeus.
haec tibi semper erunt, et cum sollemnia uota
reddemus Nymphis, et cum lustrabimus agros.
dum iuga montis aper, fluuios dum piscis amabit,
dumque thymo pascentur apes, dum rore cicadae,
semper honos nomenque tuum laudesque manebunt.
ut Baccho Cererique, tibi sic uota quotannis
agricolae facient: damnabis tu quoque uotis.

MOPSUS

Quae tibi, quae tali reddam pro carmine dona?
nam neque me tantum uenientis sibilus Austri
nec percussa iuuant fluctu tam litora, nec quae
saxosas inter decurrunt flumina uallis.

MENALCAS

Hac te nos fragili donabimus ante cicuta;
haec nos 'formosum Corydon ardebat Alexin',
haec eadem docuit 'cuium pecus? an Meliboei?'

'He is a god, Menalcas!' Daphnis, be kind
And bountiful to your own! Behold, I have
Established four altars here: two are for Daphnis,
Two for Apollo. Yearly I will set out
Two bowls of milk, foaming with freshness, and two
Of the richest olive oil, and best of all
For the pleasure of the feast—whether in winter,
Before the fire, or else at the autumn harvest,
Under the shade of trees—I will pour out
Nectareous Ariusian wine from Chios.
Damoetas and Lyctian Aegon will sing for us,
And Alphesiboeus will dance like a leaping satyr.
Thus will it be for you for ever more,
Both at the time of year when it's right to make
Our annual devotions to the Nymphs
And at the time of year when we bless our fields.
As long as the wild boar loves the mountain ridges,
As long as fish love swimming in the rivers,
As long as bees pasture upon the thyme fields,
Cicadas on morning dew, as long as this
The glory of Daphnis will last. Just as, each year,
Farmers make binding vows to Bacchus and Ceres,
So we will make our binding vows to you."

MOPSUS

What can I give you back for such a song?
It is more beautiful than either the first
Sounds of the South Wind in the early moments
Of Spring beginning, or sounds of waves as they break
Upon the beach, or sounds of mountain streams
Flowing downhill to the valley over stones.

MENALCAS

First I want to give you this hemlock pipe,
The one on which I learned to play the songs
"Corydon loved the fair Alexis" and
"Whose flock is this? Is it Meliboeus's flock?"

MOPSUS

At tu sume pedum, quod, me cum saepe rogaret,
non tulit Antigenes (et erat tum dignus amari),
formosum paribus nodis atque aere, Menalca.

Here is a beautiful shepherd's staff, the one
Antigenes often asked me for and was
Refused, though then he deserved my love. The knots
Are evenly spaced, the rings are brass, Menalcas.

ECLOGA VI

Prima Syracosio dignata est ludere uersu
nostra neque erubuit siluas habitare Thalea.
cum canerem reges et proelia, Cynthius aurem
uellit et admonuit: 'pastorem, Tityre, pinguis
pascere oportet ouis, deductum dicere carmen.'
nunc ego (namque super tibi erunt qui dicere laudes,
Vare, tuas cupiant et tristia condere bella)
agrestem tenui meditabor harundine Musam:
non iniussa cano. si quis tamen haec quoque, si quis
captus amore leget, te nostrae, Vare, myricae,
te nemus omne canet; nec Phoebo gratior ulla est
quam sibi quae Vari praescripsit pagina nomen.
 Pergite, Pierides. Chromis et Mnasyllos in antro
Silenum pueri somno uidere iacentem,
inflatum hesterno uenas, ut semper, Iaccho;
serta procul tantum capiti delapsa iacebant
et grauis attrita pendebat cantharus ansa.

ECLOGUE VI

[TITYRUS]

When I began to write, my Muse did not
Disdain to play Sicilian games nor did
She blush to live in the woods, and when I thought
Of singing of kings and battles, the god Apollo
Tweaked my ear and said to me, "A shepherd
Should feed fat sheep and sing a slender song."
So now—since there are plenty to sing your praise
And plenty to celebrate grim deeds of war—
I'll study how to play the pastoral reed
And win the favor of the country Muse.
I will not sing what I'm not supposed to sing.
But if there's anyone, captured by love, who therefore
Might be persuaded to read these lines, then, Varus,
Our tamarisks and groves will sing of you,
For nothing is more pleasing to Apollo
Than the name of Varus on the title page.

Let the Pierian maidens begin the story:

There were two young boys, Chromis and Mnasyllos,
Who happened upon Silenus where he lay,
Veiny and swollen with wine as usual,
Sleeping it off in a cave; on the ground nearby
Were the garlands fallen off his drunken head
And his tankard atilt and hanging from his hand.

adgressi (nam saepe senex spe carminis ambo
luserat) iniciunt ipsis ex uincula sertis.
addit se sociam timidisque superuenit Aegle,
Aegle Naiadum pulcherrima, iamque uidenti
sanguineis frontem moris et tempora pingit.
ille dolum ridens 'quo uincula nectitis?' inquit;
'soluite me, pueri; satis est potuisse uideri.
carmina quae uultis cognoscite; carmina uobis,
huic aliud mercedis erit.' simul incipit ipse.
tum uero in numerum Faunosque ferasque uideres
ludere, tum rigidas motare cacumina quercus;
nec tantum Phoebo gaudet Parnasia rupes,
nec tantum Rhodope miratur et Ismarus Orphea.

 Namque canebat uti magnum per inane coacta
semina terrarumque animaeque marisque fuissent
et liquidi simul ignis; ut his ex omnia primis,
omnia et ipse tener mundi concreuerit orbis;
tum durare solum et discludere Nerea ponto
coeperit et rerum paulatim sumere formas;
iamque nouum terrae stupeant lucescere solem,
altius atque cadant summotis nubibus imbres,
incipiant siluae cum primum surgere cumque
rara per ignaros errent animalia montis.
hinc lapides Pyrrhae iactos, Saturnia regna,
Caucasiasque refert uolucris furtumque Promethei.

So the two boys tied him up with his own garlands,
Because he hadn't kept the promise he'd made,
To sing a song or two. Along came Aegle,
Aegle who was the prettiest of the Naiads,
And Aegle helped the timid boys to paint
Silenus' face with bright red mulberry juice,
Just as he waked. Silenus laughed at the joke
They'd played on him, and said, "Come on, boys,
Turn me loose. Why have you tied me up?
Now that you've shown your power, I'll sing the songs.
Aegle will have another kind of prize."
With that he began to sing, and right away
Fauns and wild beasts keeping the meter danced,
And rigid oak trees nodded their heads to the music.
The rocks on Apollo's Parnassus were not more joyful
Nor Orpheus' Rhodope more full of wonder.

His singing begins with the story of how the seeds
Of earth, and air, and water, and flowing fire
Were brought together through the vast inane
And how from these events all things began.
He sang of how the newborn orb of the world
Began to coalesce, and how the ground
Began to harden, and how it was that the rule
Of the god of the sea was confined to the sea, and how
The earth looked up in wonder at the new
Light of the shining sun, and how from clouds
The rain came down in showers; then woods arose,
And living creatures wandered on the sides
Of mountains unaware of what they were.

Then he tells other stories: the one about
The stones that Pyrrha threw becoming the women
From whom the human race began again
After the Flood subsided; he told the story
Of Saturn's reign; the story of how Prometheus
Was chained on the mountain because he stole the fire,

his adiungit, Hylan nautae quo fonte relictum
clamassent, ut litus 'Hyla, Hyla' omne sonaret;
et fortunatam, si numquam armenta fuissent,
Pasiphaen niuei solatur amore iuuenci.
a, uirgo infelix, quae te dementia cepit!
Proetides implerunt falsis mugitibus agros,
at non tam turpis pecudum tamen ulla secuta
concubitus, quamuis collo timuisset aratrum
et saepe in leui quaesisset cornua fronte.
a! uirgo infelix, tu nunc in montibus erras:
ille latus niueum molli fultus hyacintho
ilice sub nigra pallentis ruminat herbas
aut aliquam in magno sequitur grege. 'claudite, Nymphae,
Dictaeae Nymphae, nemorum iam claudite saltus,
si qua forte ferant oculis sese obuia nostris
errabunda bouis uestigia; forsitan illum
aut herba captum uiridi aut armenta secutum
perducant aliquae stabula ad Gortynia uaccae.'
tum canit Hesperidum miratam mala puellam;
tum Phaethontiadas musco circumdat amarae
corticis atque solo proceras erigit alnos.
tum canit, errantem Permessi ad flumina Gallum
Aonas in montis ut duxerit una sororum,
utque uiro Phoebi chorus adsurrexerit omnis;
ut Linus haec illi diuino carmine pastor

And vultures ate his liver over and over.
He told the story of how the sailors called out
To Hylas "Hylas! Hylas!" left behind
Where he went to fetch the water from a spring
And "Hylas! Hylas!" echoed back to them.
In pity he sings the tale of Pasiphaë—
She would have been lucky if there had never been cattle—
Who hopelessly fell in love with a snow-white bull.
Ah, poor unhappy maiden, what was this madness?
Proetus' maddened daughters thought they were cows;
Their mooing filled the fields as if they were;
And yet, though in her madness each of them feared
The yoke about her neck and often fingered
Her smooth brow for the signs of bovine horns,
There wasn't one of them who ever really
Desired vile copulation with a beast.
Ah, poor unhappy maiden, now you wander
Alone somewhere in the hills; meanwhile, the bull
Couching his snow-white flank on hyacinth flowers
Lies in the shade of the ilex, chewing pale grasses,
Or follows after some heifer in the herd.
"Dictaean Nymphs," cries out Pasiphaë,
"Surround the upland pastures and close them in.
It may be that I'll see his hoofprint signs.
It may be that some meadow down below
Will tempt him or the sight of cows in the herd
As they come home will lead him down to our stables."

Next he sang about Atalanta's wonder
At seeing the apples of the Hesperides;
And then his music changes Phaëton's sisters
To grieving poplars, weeping amber tears.
And then he sings of Calliope and how,
When finding Gallus wandering by the river,
She led him up to the top of Helicon
And there Apollo's chorus got to their feet
To honor him, and Linus the shepherd singer,

floribus atque apio crinis ornatus amaro
dixerit: 'hos tibi dant calamos (en accipe) Musae,
Ascraeo quos ante seni, quibus ille solebat
cantando rigidas deducere montibus ornos.
his tibi Grynei nemoris dicatur origo,
ne quis sit lucus quo se plus iactet Apollo.'
 Quid loquar aut Scyllam Nisi, quam fama secuta est
candida succinctam latrantibus inguina monstris
Dulichias uexasse rates et gurgite in alto
a! timidos nautas canibus lacerasse marinis;
aut ut mutatos Terei narrauerit artus,
quas illi Philomela dapes, quae dona pararit,
quo cursu deserta petiuerit et quibus ante
infelix sua tecta super uolitauerit alis?
omnia, quae Phoebo quondam meditante beatus
audiit Eurotas iussitque ediscere lauros,
ille canit, pulsae referunt ad sidera ualles;
cogere donec ouis stabulis numerumque referre
iussit et inuito processit Vesper Olympo.

Wearing a crown of flowers and bitter parsley,
Offered to Gallus a pipe made out of reeds
That once upon a time the Muses gave
To Hesiod whose singing brought the ash trees
Down the mountainside to hear his music,
And Linus said, "Receive these reeds and with them
Make music of the story of how the grove
Called Gryneum came to be the most favored place
Of all the places favored by Apollo."

He told the story of Scylla, Nisus's daughter,
The story often told, about how she
With yelling monsters whirling around her hips
Harassed the wallowing ships of Ithaca,
And oh! her sea-hounds tore to bits and pieces
The bodies of hysterical Ithacan sailors
Pulled down and whelmed in that devouring vortex.
He told about the king who married Procne,
And what the dinner was her sister served him,
And whose was the head she showed him at the table,
And how she fled to the desert, and after that,
What bird she had become, poor thing, that hovers
With fluttering wings above the roof of her house.

All of the songs Apollo sang alongside
The listening river Eurotas who, blessed with the music,
Commanded that his laurels learn them by heart,
All these Silenus sang; the echoing valleys
Echoed them up to the stars, till the Evening Star
Said it was time for the flocks to come back in,
Time to be counted, and time for him to set out
Over a sky reluctant to yield the day.

ECLOGA VII

[MELIBOEUS / CORYDON / THYRSIS]

MELIBOEUS

Forte sub arguta consederat ilice Daphnis,
compulerantque greges Corydon et Thyrsis in unum,
Thyrsis ouis, Corydon distentas lacte capellas,
ambo florentes aetatibus, Arcades ambo,
et cantare pares et respondere parati.
huc mihi, dum teneras defendo a frigore myrtos,
uir gregis ipse caper deerrauerat; atque ego Daphnin
aspicio. ille ubi me contra uidet, 'ocius' inquit
'huc ades, o Meliboee; caper tibi saluus et haedi;
et, si quid cessare potes, requiesce sub umbra.
huc ipsi potum uenient per prata iuuenci,
hic uiridis tenera praetexit harundine ripas
Mincius, eque sacra resonant examina quercu.'
quid facerem? neque ego Alcippen nec Phyllida habebam
depulsos a lacte domi quae clauderet agnos,
et certamen erat, Corydon cum Thyrside, magnum;

ECLOGUE VII

[MELIBOEUS / DAPHNIS / CORYDON / THYRSIS]

MELIBOEUS

Daphnis, one day, was sitting in the shade
Of a murmuring ilex tree, and Corydon
And Thyrsis, both nearby, were tending their flocks,
Thyrsis his sheep and Corydon his she-goats,
Their udders swollen with milk. Thyrsis and he
Were both like flowers in bloom, the two of them,
Arcadians both, and ready to compete
With song replying to song replying to song.
And I was a little way off, mulching the roots
Of my myrtle plants to keep them from the cold.
My billy goat, the boss man of my flock,
Had wandered away somewhere, away from the others.
Then I saw Daphnis and Daphnis caught sight of me
And he called out, "O Meliboeus, come here,
Come here and sit in the shade, and rest yourself.
Your goats and kids are perfectly safe and sound;
Your oxen will come this way all by themselves
Across the fields and down to the stream to drink
From Mincius' cool waters where the reeds
Flower along the riverbanks and where
The bees are humming around the ancient oak."
I thought, why not? I have no Phyllis at home
And no Alcippe to care for the just-weaned lambs,
But Corydon and Thyrsis in a contest

posthabui tamen illorum mea seria ludo.
alternis igitur contendere uersibus ambo
coepere, alternos Musae meminisse uolebant.
hos Corydon, illos referebat in ordine Thyrsis.

CORYDON

Nymphae noster amor Libethrides, aut mihi carmen,
quale meo Codro, concedite (proxima Phoebi
uersibus ille facit) aut, si non possumus omnes,
hic arguta sacra pendebit fistula pinu.

THYRSIS

Pastores, hedera crescentem ornate poetam,
Arcades, inuidia rumpantur ut ilia Codro;
aut, si ultra placitum laudarit, baccare frontem
cingite, ne uati noceat mala lingua futuro.

CORYDON

Saetosi caput hoc apri tibi, Delia, paruus
et ramosa Micon uiuacis cornua cerui.
si proprium hoc fuerit, leui de marmore tota
puniceo stabis suras euincta coturno.

THYRSIS

Sinum lactis et haec te liba, Priape, quotannis
exspectare sat est: custos es pauperis horti.
nunc te marmoreum pro tempore fecimus; at tu,
si fetura gregem suppleuerit, aureus esto.

CORYDON

Nerine Galatea, thymo mihi dulcior Hyblae,
candidior cycnis, hedera formosior alba,

Is a contest not to miss. I thought, this game
Takes precedence over work, and so I stayed.
And so the two began the contest, each of them
Taking his turn as the Muses brought to mind
The alternate verses, Corydon first, then Thyrsis.

<div style="text-align:center">CORYDON</div>

"Beloved Nymphs of Helicon, grant me
Such power as you have granted Codrus, whose
Music comes closest to Apollo's music;
If this should not be granted, then will I
Hang up my shepherd's pipe on this pine-tree bough."

<div style="text-align:center">THYRSIS</div>

"Arcadian shepherds, crown your newborn poet;
Let Codrus burst with envy; or, if he
Should choose to overpraise me, bind my brow
With a foxglove garland to guard me from any harm
That comes toward me from his palavering."

<div style="text-align:center">CORYDON</div>

"Delia, goddess, Micon offers to you
This bristling head of a wild boar and the branching
Antlers of a full-grown stag. If all
Goes well, we promise we'll fashion your statue for you,
In shining marble and purple hunting boots."

<div style="text-align:center">THYRSIS</div>

"Priapus, these cakes and a bowl of milk are all
You can hope to get each year; the garden's poor;
You're only made of stone right now, but if
The births go well and many lambs are born
We'll put up a statue of you made out of gold."

<div style="text-align:center">CORYDON</div>

"O Galatea, sweeter to me than is
The thyme that blooms at Hybla, whiter than swansdown,

cum primum pasti repetent praesepia tauri,
si qua tui Corydonis habet te cura, uenito.

<center>THYRSIS</center>

Immo ego Sardoniis uidear tibi amarior herbis,
horridior rusco, proiecta uilior alga,
si mihi non haec lux toto iam longior anno est.
ite domum pasti, si quis pudor, ite iuuenci.

<center>CORYDON</center>

Muscosi fontes et somno mollior herba,
et quae uos rara uiridis tegit arbutus umbra,
solstitium pecori defendite: iam uenit aestas
torrida, iam lento turgent in palmite gemmae.

<center>THYRSIS</center>

Hic focus et taedae pingues, hic plurimus ignis
semper, et adsidua postes fuligine nigri.
hic tantum Boreae curamus frigora quantum
aut numerum lupus aut torrentia flumina ripas.

<center>CORYDON</center>

Stant et iuniperi et castaneae hirsutae,
strata iacent passim sua quaeque sub arbore poma,
omnia nunc rident: at si formosus Alexis
montibus his abeat, uideas et flumina sicca.

<center>THYRSIS</center>

Aret ager, uitio moriens sitit aëris herba,
Liber pampineas inuidit collibus umbras:

Lovelier than the palest ivy, if
You care for Corydon, come here to him,
When the cattle come in at evening from the pastures."

THYRSIS

"If this day seem any shorter to me than a year,
Then let me be no better to Phyllis than seaweed,
Sharper than thorns, bitterer than the herbs
They grow in Sardinia. So get along, cows,
Get home, get home, you've eaten your fill in the fields."

CORYDON

"You mossy spring, you grasses softer than sleep,
Under the shade cast by the little tree,
Protect my flock from the scorching heat of noon.
Summer is coming on. The buds begin
To swell and cluster on the spreading vines."

THYRSIS

"We have a hearth with a fire that's always going,
Fed with resiny pinelogs from the woods;
Doorposts black with soot; we're bothered by
The winter cold no more than wolves by sheep
Or torrents by the banks that try to hold them."

CORYDON

"We've juniper trees and chestnut trees, and such
Abundance that the ground is covered with
What falls from the loaded boughs; a smiling scene;
But if Alexis should desert these hills,
The flowing streams would shrivel and run dry."

THYRSIS

"The field is dry; in the blighted air the grass
Is dying for lack of water; Bacchus denies
The shade of his vines to the arid hill; but when

Phyllidis aduentu nostrae nemus omne uirebit,
Iuppiter et laeto descendet plurimus imbri.

Populus Alcidae gratissima, uitis Iaccho,
formosae myrtus Veneri, sua laurea Phoebo;
Phyllis amat corylos: illas dum Phyllis amabit,
nec myrtus uincet corylos, nec laurea Phoebi.

Fraxinus in siluis pulcherrima, pinus in hortis,
populus in fluuiis, abies in montibus altis:
saepius at si me, Lycida formose, reuisas,
fraxinus in siluis cedat tibi, pinus in hortis.

Haec memini, et uictum frustra contendere Thyrsin.
ex illo Corydon Corydon est tempore nobis.

My Phyllis returns, then green returns to the woods
As Jupiter descends in generous showers."

CORYDON

"The poplar is most pleasing to Alcides,
The vine to Bacchus; Apollo loves the laurel,
And Venus the myrtle. While Phyllis loves the hazel,
Neither the myrtle that Venus loves nor Apollo's
Laurel outdoes the hazel that Phyllis loves."

THYRSIS

"The ash tree is the most beautiful in the woods,
The pine in gardens, the poplar by the river,
The fir tree high in the mountains, but Lycidas,
If you return, the ash tree in the woods,
The pine tree, all, yield precedence to you."

MELIBOEUS

I remember how the contest went, how Thyrsis,
Striving to win, was the loser, and since that time
It has been Corydon's, Corydon's name we cry.

ECLOGA VIII

[DAMON / ALPHESIBOEUS]

Pastorum Musam Damonis et Alphesiboei,
immemor herbarum quos est mirata iuuenca
certantis, quorum stupefactae carmine lynces,
et mutata suos requierunt flumina cursus,
Damonis Musam dicemus et Alphesiboei.
tu mihi, seu magni superas iam saxa Timaui
siue oram Illyrici legis aequoris,—en erit umquam
ille dies, mihi cum liceat tua dicere facta?
en erit ut liceat totum mihi ferre per orbem
sola Sophocleo tua carmina digna coturno?
a te principium, tibi desinam: accipe iussis
carmina coepta tuis, atque hanc sine tempora circum
inter uictricis hederam tibi serpere lauros.
 Frigida uix caelo noctis decesserat umbra,
cum ros in tenera pecori gratissimus herba:
incumbens tereti Damon sic coepit oliuae.

ECLOGUE VIII

[VIRGIL / DAMON / ALPHESIBOEUS]

VIRGIL

The Muse of the shepherds Alphesiboeus and Damon,
At whose contending songs the very cattle
Were spellbound in the field, forgetting to graze—
The lynx was spellbound too, hearing the music—
And the rivers, spellbound, stood still listening—
I sing the Muse of Damon and Alphesiboeus.
Whether it be that you are passing by
The great rocks at the mouth of the river Timavus
Or sailing homeward along the Illyrian coast,
I long for the day when I shall be able to sing
In celebration of your victories,
And celebrate to all the world as well
Your Sophoclean music. These songs of mine,
In my beginning, are for you; and when
I come to the end, it shall be in your service.
Accept these songs written at your command;
May these few ivy leaves be among your laurels.

The cool shadows of night had scarcely gone
Away from the morning sky, just at the time
When the dew on the tender grass most pleases the flock,
When, leaning on his elegant olive-staff,
Damon began his song:

Nascere praeque diem ueniens age, Lucifer, almum,
coniugis indigno Nysae deceptus amore
dum queror et diuos, quamquam nil testibus illis
profeci, extrema moriens tamen adloquor hora.
 incipe Maenalios mecum, mea tibia, uersus.
Maenalus argutumque nemus pinusque loquentis
semper habet, semper pastorum ille audit amores
Panaque, qui primus calamos non passus inertis.
 incipe Maenalios mecum, mea tibia, uersus.
Mopso Nysa datur: quid non speremus amantes?
iungentur iam grypes equis, aeuoque sequenti
cum canibus timidi uenient ad pocula dammae.
 incipe Maenalios mecum, mea tibia, uersus.
Mopse, nouas incide faces: tibi ducitur uxor.
sparge, marite, nuces: tibi deserit Hesperus Oetam.
 incipe Maenalios mecum, mea tibia, uersus.
o digno coniuncta uiro, dum despicis omnis,
dumque tibi est odio mea fistula dumque capellae
hirsutumque supercilium promissaque barba,
nec curare deum credis mortalia quemquam.
 incipe Maenalios mecum, mea tibia, uersus.
saepibus in nostris paruam te roscida mala
(dux ego uester eram) uidi cum matre legentem.
alter ab undecimo tum me iam acceperat annus,
iam fragilis poteram a terra contingere ramos:
ut uidi, ut perii, ut me malus abstulit error!
 incipe Maenalios mecum, mea tibia, uersus.
nunc scio quid sit Amor: nudis in cautibus illum
aut Tmaros aut Rhodope aut extremi Garamantes
nec generis nostri puerum nec sanguinis edunt.

"Arise, O star

That greets the brightening day, while I lament
Because my sworn love Nysa has deceived me;
Although no help has come for me from them,
I call on the gods to witness as I die.
 My flute, begin to play Maenalus' song.
There's music in the groves that grow upon
The sides of Mount Maenalus, music of Pan,
Who first called music forth from silent reeds,
The songs of shepherds telling of their loves.
 My flute, begin to play Maenalus' song.
Nysa given to Mopsus! What is it that
Lovers can hope for? Griffins and mares will mate,
And in the next age the timid doe will come
Down to the stream to drink along with dogs.
 My flute, begin to play Maenalus' song.
Let them light up the torches, Mopsus, they
Are bringing you your bride. The Evening Star
Is rising for you now from behind the mountain.
 My flute, begin to play Maenalus' song.
That she, who scorned all men, and scorned my goats,
My shepherd's flute, my shaggy beard and eyebrows,
And thought the gods cared nothing for anything human,
That she should be the bride of such as him!
 My flute, begin to play Maenalus' song.
I saw you, when you were a little child.
Your mother was with you. I led you to the place
In our garden where there was the apple tree,
With dewy apples growing on the boughs.
I was just going on twelve, just tall enough
To reach up to the branches to pick the apples.
I saw, I saw, and I was lost forever.
 My flute, begin to play Maenalus' song.
I know what Love is. He was born on the rocks
Of Tmaros or of Rhodope or else
Far in the Garamantian Desert. Love

incipe Maenalios mecum, mea tibia, uersus.
saeuus Amor docuit natorum sanguine matrem
commaculare manus; crudelis tu quoque, mater.
crudelis mater magis, an puer improbus ille?
improbus ille puer; crudelis tu quoque, mater.
 incipe Maenalios mecum, mea tibia, uersus.
nunc et ouis ultro fugiat lupus, aurea durae
mala ferant quercus, narcisso floreat alnus,
pinguia corticibus sudent electra myricae,
certent et cycnis ululae, sit Tityrus Orpheus,
Orpheus in siluis, inter delphinas Arion.
 incipe Maenalios mecum, mea tibia, uersus.
omnia uel medium fiat mare. uiuite siluae:
praeceps aërii specula de montis in undas
deferar; extremum hoc munus morientis habeto.
 desine Maenalios, iam desine, tibia, uersus.
 Haec Damon; uos, quae responderit Alphesiboeus,
dicite, Pierides: non omnia possumus omnes.

ALPHESIBOEUS

 Effer aquam et molli cinge haec altaria uitta
uerbenasque adole pinguis et mascula tura,
coniugis ut magicis sanos auertere sacris
experiar sensus; nihil hic nisi carmina desunt.
 ducite ab urbe domum, mea carmina, ducite Daphnin.
carmina uel caelo possunt deducere lunam,
carminibus Circe socios mutauit Ulixi,
frigidus in pratis cantando rumpitur anguis.
 ducite ab urbe domum, mea carmina, ducite Daphnin.
terna tibi haec primum triplici diuersa colore

Is not of our blood and he is not of our kind.
My flute, begin to play Maenalus' song.
Love taught a mother how to stain her hands
With the blood of her children. Tell me, Mother, which
Of the two of you was the crueler one? Which one
Of the two, was it, Mother, cruel Love, or you?
My flute, begin to play Maenalus' song.
Let wolves run away from sheep, let golden apples
Suddenly be the fruit of mighty oaks,
Narcissus bloom on the boughs of alder trees,
And amber ooze from the bark of tamarisks;
Let owls compete with swans, and Tityrus
Compete with Orpheus—an Orpheus of the woods,
Let Tityrus be Arion among the dolphins.
My flute, begin to play Maenalus' song.
Farewell to woods, let all be ocean now.
Headlong I'll fall to my death from this high cliff.
My song be my last offering to you.
Thus ends, my flute, the song of Maenalus."

VIRGIL

Thus Damon's song. Pierian maidens, come,
Help me to tell how Alphesiboeus replied.

ALPHESIBOEUS

"Bring water, and bring the ribbons of softest wool
To wind around the altar, and light the fire
Of aromatic woods and frankincense
To make the incense smoke, and I will with
Such magic strive to change my lover's mind.
All that is needful now is a charm to sing.
Bring Daphnis home, bring Daphnis home, my charms.
Charms can entice the moon down out of the sky;
Ulysses' men were changed by Circe's charms;
Charms can cause the snake in the field to burst.
Bring Daphnis home, bring Daphnis home, my charms.
I weave the threads around your image thrice,

licia circumdo, terque haec altaria circum
effigiem duco; numero deus impare gaudet.

 ducite ab urbe domum, mea carmina, ducite Daphnin.
necte tribus nodis ternos, Amarylli, colores;
necte, Amarylli, modo et 'Veneris' dic 'uincula necto'.

 ducite ab urbe domum, mea carmina, ducite Daphnin.
limus ut hic durescit, et haec ut cera liquescit
uno eodemque igni, sic nostro Daphnis amore.
sparge molam et fragilis incende bitumine lauros:
Daphnis me malus urit, ego hanc in Daphnide laurum.

 ducite ab urbe domum, mea carmina, ducite Daphnin.
talis amor Daphnin qualis cum fessa iuuencum
per nemora atque altos quaerendo bucula lucos
propter aquae riuum uiridi procumbit in ulua
perdita, nec serae meminit decedere nocti,
talis amor teneat, nec sit mihi cura mederi.

 ducite ab urbe domum, mea carmina, ducite Daphnin.
has olim exuuias mihi perfidus ille reliquit,
pignora cara sui, quae nunc ego limine in ipso,
Terra, tibi mando; debent haec pignora Daphnin.

 ducite ab urbe domum, mea carmina, ducite Daphnin.
has herbas atque haec Ponto mihi lecta uenena
ipse dedit Moeris (nascuntur plurima Ponto);
his ego saepe lupum fieri et se condere siluis
Moerim, saepe animas imis excire sepulcris,
atque satas alio uidi traducere messis.

 ducite ab urbe domum, mea carmina, ducite Daphnin.

Three-colored threads, and carry the image thrice
Around the altar, for the god loves threes.
 Bring Daphnis home, bring Daphnis home, my charms.
Weave, Amaryllis, weave, three threads around,
And make three times three-colored knots, and say
'With these three threads I weave the chains of love.'
 Bring Daphnis home, bring Daphnis home, my charms.
As in one fire this image made of clay
Grows hard and this of wax grows soft, so may
The heart of Daphnis melt for love of me.
Cast meal about, light bitumen pitch and burn
The crackling laurel boughs; Daphnis burns me;
Thus in the laurel fire may Daphnis melt.
 Bring Daphnis home, bring Daphnis home, my charms.
May he be seized by such desire as that
Of a lovesick heifer longing for her bull,
Who weary and lost from following where he went
Lies down in the grass that grows beside the stream
That through the deep woods flows; weary and lost,
Forgetful of her home far into the night;
May he be seized by such desire as hers,
And I not care at all to be the cure.
 Bring Daphnis home, bring Daphnis home, my charms.
These garments he, perfidious, left as pledges;
Now I commit them, earth, to you before
The threshold of my house; these garments are
The pledges that my Daphnis belongs to me.
 Bring Daphnis home, bring Daphnis home, my charms.
Moeris gave me these herbs and poison plants
That come from Pontus, where they grow aplenty.
How often I have seen how by their aid
He turned into a wolf loping away
Into the woods, and I have seen him use them
To call up ghosts out of their graves, or cause
The seeds one farmer just put down in his field
To fly away at night to grow in another's.
 Bring Daphnis home, bring Daphnis home, my charms.

fer cineres, Amarylli, foras riuoque fluenti
transque caput iace, nec respexeris. his ego Daphnin
adgrediar; nihil ille deos, nil carmina curat.

 ducite ab urbe domum, mea carmina, ducite Daphnin.
'aspice: corripuit tremulis altaria flammis
sponte sua, dum ferre moror, cinis ipse. bonum sit!'
nescio quid certe est, et Hylax in limine latrat.
credimus? an, qui amant, ipsi sibi somnia fingunt?

 parcite, ab urbe uenit, iam parcite carmina, Daphnis.

Now, Amaryllis, take the embers out
And carry them to a stream, and turn around,
And throw them over your shoulder into the stream,
And don't look back. Thus will I win back Daphnis,
Who doesn't know what gods and charms can do.

> *Bring Daphnis home, bring Daphnis home, my charms.*

O see! before they're carried out the ashes
Suddenly, of their own accord, burst forth,
And the altar burns once more with quivering flames.
Let this be good. —I think it may be good.
The dog is barking down by the front gate.
Can I believe it, or is it that lovers dream?

> *Cease now, my charms, my Daphnis has come home!"*

ECLOGA IX

[LYCIDAS / MOERIS]

LYCIDAS

Quo te, Moeri, pedes? an, quo uia ducit, in urbem?

MOERIS

O Lycida, uiui peruenimus, aduena nostri
(quod numquam ueriti sumus) ut possessor agelli
diceret: 'haec mea sunt; ueteres migrate coloni.'
nunc uicti, tristes, quoniam fors omnia uersat,
hos illi (quod nec uertat bene) mittimus haedos.

LYCIDAS

Certe equidem audieram, qua se subducere colles
incipiunt mollique iugum demittere cliuo,
usque ad aquam et ueteres, iam fracta cacumina, fagos,
omnia carminibus uestrum seruasse Menalcan.

MOERIS

Audieras, et fama fuit; sed carmina tantum
nostra ualent, Lycida, tela inter Martia quantum
Chaonias dicunt aquila ueniente columbas.
quod nisi me quacumque nouas incidere lites

ECLOGUE IX

[LYCIDAS / MOERIS]

LYCIDAS

Moeris, why are you taking the path to town?

MOERIS

O Lycidas, we never thought that what
Has happened to us was ever going to happen,
And now we've lived to see it. A stranger came
To take possession of our farm, and said:
"I own this place; you have to leave this place."
Heartbroken and beaten, since fortune will have it so,
I have to carry these kids to him in town.
I only hope bad luck for him goes with them.

LYCIDAS

But I was told Menalcas with his songs
Had saved the land, from where those hills arise
To where they slope down gently to the water,
Near those old beech trees, with their broken tops.

MOERIS

Yes, that was the story; but what can music do
Against the weapons of soldiers? When eagles come,
Tell me what doves can possibly do about it?

ante sinistra caua monuisset ab ilice cornix,
nec tuus hic Moeris nec uiueret ipse Menalcas.

LYCIDAS

Heu, cadit in quemquam tantum scelus? heu, tua nobis
paene simul tecum solacia rapta, Menalca!
quis caneret Nymphas? quis humum florentibus herbis
spargeret aut uiridi fontis induceret umbra?
uel quae sublegi tacitus tibi carmina nuper,
cum te ad delicias ferres Amaryllida nostras?
'Tityre, dum redeo (breuis est uia), pasce capellas,
et potum pastas age, Tityre, et inter agendum
occursare capro (cornu ferit ille) caueto.'

MOERIS

Immo haec, quae Varo necdum perfecta canebat:
'Vare, tuum nomen, superet modo Mantua nobis,
Mantua uae miserae nimium uicina Cremonae,
cantantes sublime ferent ad sidera cycni.'

LYCIDAS

Sic tua Cyrneas fugiant examina taxos,
sic cytiso pastae distendant ubera uaccae,
incipe, si quid habes. et me fecere poetam
Pierides, sunt et mihi carmina, me quoque dicunt
uatem pastores; sed non ego credulus illis.
nam neque adhuc Vario uideor nec dicere Cinna
digna, sed argutos inter strepere anser olores.

If the raven on the left in this hollow oak
Hadn't warned me not to resist, I might have been killed.
Menalcas himself might very well have been killed.

<center>LYCIDAS</center>

Oh, how did this calamity befall us?
Alas, the solace that your music brought us,
Was it so nearly lost to us, Menalcas?
Who else would sing of the Nymphs? And who would scatter
The wildflowers on the ground or shade the springs
With the green shade of trees? And who would sing
Such songs as the one I overheard one day
That you were singing as you were setting off
To visit Amaryllis, our delight:
"Tityrus, while I'm gone, please feed my goats
(I won't be gone for long), and when you've fed them,
Please drive them down to the water, and when you do,
Be careful of the billy goat; he butts."

<center>MOERIS</center>

Yes, and then that poem, addressed to Varus,
Though not completed as yet: "Varus, your name—
If Mantua can be spared, our Mantua,
Alas, too close to woeful Cremona—the swans,
Singing, will carry your name up to the stars."

<center>LYCIDAS</center>

So that your cows may feast on clover grass,
That makes their udders prosper and be more ample,
And so that your bees may avoid the Corsican yews,
If you have any song to sing, begin.
The Pierian maidens have made me a poet too,
For I have songs; the shepherds call me a poet;
But I don't really believe them, at least not yet.
Nothing I've sung so far is good enough
For Varius or Cinna to listen to.
My songs are honking geese among the swans.

MOERIS

Id quidem ago et tacitus, Lycida, mecum ipse uoluto,
si ualeam meminisse; neque est ignobile carmen.
'huc ades, o Galatea; quis est nam ludus in undis?
hic uer purpureum, uarios hic flumina circum
fundit humus flores, hic candida populus antro
imminet et lentae texunt umbracula uites.
huc ades; insani feriant sine litora fluctus.'

LYCIDAS

Quid, quae te pura solum sub nocte canentem
audieram? numeros memini, si uerba tenerem:
'Daphni, quid antiquos signorum suspicis ortus?
ecce Dionaei processit Caesaris astrum,
astrum quo segetes gauderent frugibus et quo
duceret apricis in collibus uua colorem.
insere, Daphni, piros: carpent tua poma nepotes.'

MOERIS

Omnia fert aetas, animum quoque. saepe ego longos
cantando puerum memini me condere soles.
nunc oblita mihi tot carmina, uox quoque Moerim
iam fugit ipsa: lupi Moerim uidere priores.
sed tamen ista satis referet tibi saepe Menalcas.

LYCIDAS

Causando nostros in longum ducis amores.
et nunc omne tibi stratum silet aequor, et omnes,
aspice, uentosi ceciderunt murmuris aurae.
hinc adeo media est nobis uia; namque sepulcrum

Lycidas, I have been saying the words of a song,
Over and over, trying to bring them back . . .
It's a good old song . . . "O Galatea, come . . .
O come away to me. Come from the sea . . .
What pleasure is there, there? . . . The spring is here . . .
Earth scatters her many varied flowers here . . . ,
And here the poplar leans above the grotto . . .
Where grapevine tendrils laced create a shade . . .
O let the waves crash raging on the shore."

What was that song I heard you singing, alone,
The other night, under a cloudless sky?
I'd remember the tune . . . if I could remember the words . . .
". . . Daphnis . . . tell me . . . why are you gazing only
At those old constellations in the sky? . . .
Look, Venus's grandson Caesar's star is rising . . .
The star that brings such joy to the ripening grain . . .
And deepens the colors of grapes on the sunny vines.
. . . Daphnis, plant your pear trees . . . years from now
The children of your children will gather the pears . . ."

Time takes all we have away from us;
I remember when I was a boy I used to sing
Every long day of summer down to darkness,
And now I am forgetting all my songs;
My voice grows hoarse; I must have been seen by a wolf.
Menalcas will sing the songs for you, when he comes.

The more you put me off the more I long
To hear the songs. See, how for you the waves
Make themselves quiet as they come in to shore.
The murmuring of the breeze is utterly stilled.
We're halfway on our journey to the town;

incipit apparere Bianoris. hic, ubi densas
agricolae stringunt frondes, hic, Moeri, canamus;
hic haedos depone, tamen ueniemus in urbem.
aut si nox pluuiam ne colligat ante ueremur,
cantantes licet usque (minus uia laedet) eamus;
cantantes ut eamus, ego hoc te fasce leuabo.

<div align="center">MOERIS</div>

Desine plura, puer, et quod nunc instat agamus;
carmina tum melius, cum uenerit ipse, canemus.

The sepulchre of Bianor is just ahead;
See where the laborers there have pruned the trees.
Moeris, let's stop here and sing our songs.
Put down the baby goats; we'll make it to town;
Or if you're afraid it's going to rain tonight,
Let's keep on going, but singing as we go.
Singing makes the journey easier.
I'll carry the basket awhile, so you can sing.

MOERIS

No more of that; let's just go on our way.
The time for singing will be when Menalcas comes.

ECLOGA X

Extremum hunc, Arethusa, mihi concede laborem:
pauca meo Gallo, sed quae legat ipsa Lycoris,
carmina sunt dicenda; neget quis carmina Gallo?
sic tibi, cum fluctus subterlabere Sicanos,
Doris amara suam non intermisceat undam,
incipe: sollicitos Galli dicamus amores,
dum tenera attondent simae uirgulta capellae.
non canimus surdis, respondent omnia siluae.

 Quae nemora aut qui uos saltus habuere, puellae
Naides, indigno cum Gallus amore peribat?
nam neque Parnasi uobis iuga, nam neque Pindi
ulla moram fecere, neque Aonie Aganippe.
illum etiam lauri, etiam fleuere myricae,
pinifer illum etiam sola sub rupe iacentem
Maenalus et gelidi fleuerunt saxa Lycaei.
stant et oues circum; nostri nec paenitet illas,
nec te paeniteat pecoris, diuine poeta:

ECLOGUE X

[VIRGIL / GALLUS]

Help me, Arethusa, to complete
This my last task, a song to sing for Gallus,
And for Lycoris to read. Let us begin,
Lest, flowing beneath the briny waters of
The ocean off the coast of Sicily,
Your purest waters mingle with the salt.
Let us together tell the sorrowful story
Of Gallus's troubles in love and of his anguish.
The snub-nosed goats nearby are cropping the grass;
The listening woods are echoing all our music.

What places do you now frequent, you Naiads,
While Gallus lies here stricken by love's betrayal?
Pindus would not have hindered you from coming,
Nor would the Muses' fountain Aganippe,
Nor Mount Parnassus; even the laurels wept,
Even the tamarisks, for Gallus's sorrow;
Even the mountains, even the cold cliffs
Of Lycaeus wept for him, and the pines that grow
On Maenalus' slopes; the flock was standing still
As if transfixed in mute compassion for him.
Gallus, divine poet, be not ashamed
That the poem should call you by the name of shepherd;

et formosus ouis ad flumina pauit Adonis.
uenit et upilio, tardi uenere subulci,
uuidus hiberna uenit de glande Menalcas.
omnes 'unde amor iste' rogant 'tibi?' uenit Apollo:
'Galle, quid insanis?' inquit. 'tua cura Lycoris
perque niues alium perque horrida castra secuta est.'
uenit et agresti capitis Siluanus honore,
florentis ferulas et grandia lilia quassans.
Pan deus Arcadiae uenit, quem uidimus ipsi
sanguineis ebuli bacis minioque rubentem.
'ecquis erit modus?' inquit. 'Amor non talia curat,
nec lacrimis crudelis Amor nec gramina riuis
nec cytiso saturantur apes nec fronde capellae.'
tristis at ille 'tamen cantabitis, Arcades,' inquit
'montibus haec uestris; soli cantare periti
Arcades. o mihi tum quam molliter ossa quiescant,
uestra meos olim si fistula dicat amores!
atque utinam ex uobis unus uestrique fuissem
aut custos gregis aut maturae uinitor uuae!
certe siue mihi Phyllis siue esset Amyntas
seu quicumque furor (quid tum, si fuscus Amyntas?
et nigrae uiolae sunt et uaccinia nigra),
mecum inter salices lenta sub uite iaceret;
serta mihi Phyllis legeret, cantaret Amyntas.

Adonis the beautiful was a shepherd too,
And watched his flock as they pastured beside the river.

The shepherds came, and after them the swineherds,
And Menalcas from his task of getting ready
The fodder for the beasts for the next winter.
They asked, "What is it you are sorrowing for?"
Apollo came, and said, "What is this madness?
Gallus, Lycoris your love has left you to follow
Another lover among the rough mountain camps
And among the freezing snows." Sylvanus came,
Adorned with fennel flowers and with lilies,
And Pan, Arcadia's god, his face and body
Stained with the juice of berries as if with blood.
—We saw him painted like that, with our own eyes.—
"Ever the same," he said. "Love cares for no one.
The bees never seem to have enough of clover,
The goats never seem to have enough of leaves,
The meadows never enough of freshening water;
Love never seems to have enough of tears."

GALLUS

Then sorrowing Gallus said, "Arcadians, sing
My story to your mountains as they listen,
For you alone are skillful at such music.
My bones would rest much easier if I knew
Your songs would tell my story in days to come.
I wish I had been one among you, tending
One of your flocks or tending one of your vineyards.
Surely in Arcadia, whether my passion
Were for Amyntas or for Phyllis or another
(Since violets and hyacinths are dark,
What would it matter that Amyntas is dark?),
My love and I would be together there
Among the willows, beneath the sheltering vines;
Phyllis would gather flowers, Amyntas would sing.

hic gelidi fontes, hic mollia prata, Lycori,
hic nemus; hic ipso tecum consumerer aeuo.
nunc insanus amor duri me Martis in armis
tela inter media atque aduersos detinet hostis.
tu procul a patria (nec sit mihi credere tantum)
Alpinas, a! dura niues et frigora Rheni
me sine sola uides. a, te ne frigora laedant!
a, tibi ne teneras glacies secet aspera plantas!
ibo et Chalcidico quae sunt mihi condita uersu
carmina pastoris Siculi modulabor auena.
certum est in siluis inter spelaea ferarum
malle pati tenerisque meos incidere amores
arboribus: crescent illae, crescetis, amores.
interea mixtis lustrabo Maenala Nymphis
aut acris uenabor apros. non me ulla uetabunt
frigora Parthenios canibus circumdare saltus.
iam mihi per rupes uideor lucosque sonantis
ire, libet Partho torquere Cydonia cornu
spicula—tamquam haec sit nostri medicina furoris,
aut deus ille malis hominum mitescere discat.
iam neque Hamadryades rursus nec carmina nobis
ipsa placent; ipsae rursus concedite siluae.
non illum nostri possunt mutare labores,
nec si frigoribus mediis Hebrumque bibamus
Sithoniasque niues hiemis subeamus aquosae,
nec si, cum moriens alta liber aret in ulmo,
Aethiopum uersemus ouis sub sidere Cancri.
omnia uincit Amor: et nos cedamus Amori.'

Lycoris, in Arcadia there are springs,
Cool as can be, and groves, and softest grass;
Together in Arcadia we would live,
And time alone could bring it to an end;
But now my maddened love of Mars the war god
Keeps me among the weapons and the foes,
And you (I cannot bear to think of it)
Are far away among the snowy Alps
Or gazing at the ice floes on the Rhine.
Oh let no harm come to her in the snows!
Oh spare her tender feet from the jagged ice!

"I will be gone from here and sing my songs
In the forest wilderness where the wild beasts are,
And carve in letters on the little trees
The story of my love, and as the trees
Will grow the letters too will grow, to cry
In a louder voice the story of my love.
I'll wander with the Nymphs or hunt wild boars
On Maenalus' side, or with my hunting dogs
I'll range the woods of cold Parthenius—
Even as I say it now I feel that I
Am joyfully roaming with my bow and arrows
High up among those cliffs and sounding groves—
But how could that be medicine for my frenzy,
Or what could teach the god of love to pity?
Nothing can change the god; now farewell, Nymphs;
No longer do our songs give pleasure now;
Farewell to the groves. No matter what we do,
No matter what hard labor, whether in winter
To drink the freezing waters of the Hebrus
And suffer Thracian sleet and blizzard winds,
Or in the summer, when the very bark
Of trees dries up and shrivels from the heat,
To tend our flocks under the sign of Cancer,
Love conquers all, and all must yield to Love."

Haec sat erit, diuae, uestrum cecinisse poetam,
dum sedet et gracili fiscellam texit hibisco,
Pierides: uos haec facietis maxima Gallo,
Gallo, cuius amor tantum mihi crescit in horas
quantum uere nouo uiridis se subicit alnus.
surgamus: solet esse grauis cantantibus umbra,
iuniperi grauis umbra; nocent et frugibus umbrae.
ite domum saturae, uenit Hesperus, ite capellae.

Enough of singing now, Pierian maidens,
While I sit here, braiding hibiscus leaves
To make a basket. These songs, because of you,
Will be approved by Gallus, Gallus for whom
My love grows hour by hour just as the young
Alder grows hour by hour in early spring.
Now we must go; the shade's not good for singers,
The juniper shade's unwholesome; unwholesome too
For the plants that need the sunshine is the shade.
Go home, my full-fed goats, you've eaten your fill,
The Evening Star is rising; it's time to go home.

Acknowledgments

I have of course consulted a number of other translations and a number of commentaries. I'm especially indebted for help with details of the translations to: H. Rushton Fairclough, ed. and trans., *Virgil*, vol. I, The Loeb Classical Library (Cambridge, Mass.: Harvard University Press, 1964, 2 vols.); Guy Lee, trans., *Virgil's Eclogues* (Liverpool: Francis Cairns, 1980); Barbara Hughes Fowler, *Virgil's Eclogues* (Chapel Hill: University of North Carolina Press, 1997); and the translation in Paul Alpers, *The Singer of the Eclogues* (Berkeley: University of California Press, 1979). I have consulted a number of commentaries and am indebted to Bruno Snell, *The Discovery of the Mind*, trans. T. G. Rosenmayr (Cambridge, Mass.: Harvard University Press, 1953); John Van Sickle, *The Design of Virgil's Bucolics* (Missoula: Scholars Press, 1978); Brooks Otis, *Virgil: A Study in Civilized Poetry* (Norman: University of Oklahoma Press, 1995); Michael Putnam, *Virgil's Pastoral Art: Studies in the Eclogues* (Princeton: Princeton University Press, 1970); Eleanor Winsor Leach, *Vergil's Eclogues: Landscapes of Experience* (Ithaca: Cornell University Press, 1974); H. J. Rose, *The Eclogues of Vergil* (Berkeley: University of California Press, 1942); Charles Martindale, ed., *The Cambridge Companion to Virgil* (Cambridge, Eng.: Cambridge University Press, 1997); Annabel Patterson, *Pastoral and Ideology: Virgil to Valéry* (Berkeley: University of California Press, 1987); Charles Segal, *Poetry and Myth in Ancient Pastoral* (Princeton: Princeton University Press, 1981). Most of all I'm indebted to Paul Alpers's two books *The Singer of the Eclogues* (previously cited) and *What Is Pastoral?* (Chicago: University of Chicago Press, 1996), and, for commentary and for notes, to Wendell Clausen, *A Commentary on Virgil, Eclogues* (Oxford: Clarendon Press, 1994).

For help with the glossary I'm indebted to J. E. Zimmerman, *Dictionary of Classical Mythology* (New York: Harper and Row, 1964).

A list of the many friends—critics and poets—who have helped and encouraged me in this project would be embarrassingly long. I am very grateful to them all, and to the editorial staff of Farrar, Straus and Giroux.

I owe special gratitude to those who have patiently answered my many questions about Virgil's Latin: Wendell Clausen, D. S. Carne-Ross, Kenneth Haynes, Rodney Dennis, Lawrence Rosenwald, Stephen Scully, and Rosanna Warren. Obviously none of these is responsible for my failures to learn from them.

Most of all I thank Anne Ferry.

I am grateful for the encouragement and financial support provided by a Fellowship from the John Simon Guggenheim Foundation (1996).

Notes

INTRODUCTION

1. Wendell Clausen, "Theocritus and Virgil," in *Cambridge History of Classical Literature*, ed. E. J. Kenney, 2 vols. (Cambridge, Eng.: Cambridge University Press, 1982), II, p. 209.
2. Paul Alpers, *What Is Pastoral?* (Chicago: University of Chicago Press, 1996), p. 169.
3. Ibid., p. 171.
4. Wendell Clausen, *A Commentary on Virgil, Eclogues* (Oxford: Clarendon Press, 1994), p. xv.
5. Alpers, *What Is Pastoral?*, pp. 137–38.
6. R. J. Tarrant, "Poetry and Power: Virgil's Poetry in Contemporary Context," in *The Cambridge Companion to Virgil*, ed. Charles Martindale (Cambridge, Eng.: Cambridge University Press, 1997), p. 173.
7. Eclogues = Selections, from the Greek word *eklegein*, "to choose." In the Middle Ages and Renaissance it was sometimes misconstrued as "goat song," derived from *aix*, "goat," and *logos*, "speech." See "Eclogue," *Princeton Encyclopedia of Poetry and Poetics*, ed. Alex Preminger and T.V.F. Brogan (Princeton: Princeton University Press, 1993), p. 317.

ECLOGUE I

The situation, as the narrative tells us, is that Meliboeus has been dispossessed of his land, as many other farmers were after Octavian's vic-

tory over Brutus and Cassius at Philippi in 42 B.C.E. They were dispossessed because Octavian needed land to give to his discharged soldiers. Meliboeus is leaving his countryside to go he knows not where. Tityrus, by contrast, who had been a slave, has finally (presumably after his spendthrift girlfriend Galatea had been succeeded by prudent Amaryllis) saved up enough money to win his freedom, and is enjoying the little piece of land he has been permitted to keep, by the "god" (probably Octavian) in Rome.

Saône: Modern name of the river Arar, in France.

that face: The face of the "young man" (Octavian).

Oaxes: A faraway river, not identified. Guy Lee's note, in his *Virgil's Eclogues* (Liverpool: Francis Cairns, 1980), says: "perhaps a conflation of the Oxus in Syria and the Araxes in Armenia."

ECLOGUE II

The poem is based on Theocritus, Idyll 11, where the singer is the grotesque lovelorn Cyclops, Polyphemus.

Alexis: "traditional name for a catamite" (Clausen's note, *A Commentary on Virgil, Eclogues*, p. 64).

ECLOGUE III

The poem derives from several Idylls of Theocritus, especially 5 but also 1, 3, 4, and 8.

Neaera: A name "associated with easy virtue" (Clausen's note, *A Commentary on Virgil, Eclogues*, p. 93).

Alcimedon: Theocritus's Idyll 5 has a bowl by Praxiteles. Alcimedon is unknown.

what was his name?: Maybe Archimedes, Sicilian mathematician and astronomer, third century B.C.E.

Bavius and Mevius: Actual poets. Nothing much is known about them. The context suggests that they are bad, and envious.

"You'll be Apollo if you can tell me where / The land is, where the sky is five feet wide." // *"Phyllis is yours if you can tell me where / The flowers bloom with royal names inscribed"*: The question of what these riddles mean has never been settled, though various explanations have been offered. See Clausen's notes on the lines (*A Commentary on Virgil, Eclogues*, pp. 116–18).

ECLOGUE IV

Wendell Clausen speaks of this poem as "brilliant and playful, with overtones of grandeur, delicate, intentionally vague perhaps—at once urgent and elusive" (*A Commentary on Virgil, Eclogues*, p. 129). It is all these things. Certainly it is the most famous of the Eclogues, partly because it was so often, especially during the Middle Ages, interpreted as a prophecy of the birth of Christ written by a Virgil who had read Isaiah and other Messianic writings.

Clausen argues that the poem was probably first written to celebrate the Pact of Brundisium between Antony and Octavian and the marriage of Antony to Octavian's sister Octavia. This was the year 40 B.C.E., when Pollio was consul, and the poem was to be understood as foretelling the peace and prosperity that would follow upon the birth of the son Antony and Octavia would have.

They had no son but Virgil had his poem. Clausen says: "Much had happened in the years after the Pact of Brundisium while Virgil was writing and rewriting his *Eclogues* and meditating his book. His consulate over, Pollio departed to govern Macedonia for Antony; Virgil was drawn into the circle of Maecenas and became acquainted with Octavian. And so, when Virgil decided to represent his epithalamium (so to call it) as an *Eclogue* and publish it, some five years later, as the fourth in his book, it is likely that he made certain changes in it, whether of addition or subtraction. Hence, it may be, something of the mystery, or mystification, of the Fourth *Eclogue*. Time obliterates: the political circumstances of the year 40 B.C., the hopes then entertained, were soon forgotten, so that in the following generation Pollio's son, the rash and ambitious Asinius Gallus, who was to die an old man in prison, could claim to be the marvellous child" (p. 126).

Sicilian Muses, sing a nobler music: The Muses have been singing "slender" pastoral songs. Sicilian = Theocritean.

a consul: Pollio was consul in 40 B.C.E.

the Sybil: The Cumaean Sibyl lived a thousand years; her dwelling was a cave at Cumae, near Naples.

the Virgin: The goddess Justice became the constellation Virgo, absenting herself from the earth as it became wicked, during the Bronze Age. Her return signals the return of the Golden Age, prophesied in this poem as being permanent.

 In later centuries, especially in the Middle Ages, this Eclogue was sometimes read, encouraged by such lines as these, as if it were a prophecy of the birth of Christ. Certainly it is possible that Virgil's reading in Messianic writings of the period—the Book of Isaiah, for example—played a part in the shaping and the tonalities of this poem.

the Age of Iron: Still worse than the Bronze Age, which was a deterioration from the Golden Age, according to Hesiod's account in *Works and Days*.

your Apollo's reign: Apollo was the patron god of the family of Julius Caesar and Octavian.

So, little baby . . . : In his commentary (pp. 123–24) Clausen cites a poem by Callimachus (*Hymn* 4), about the birth of Apollo, and two poems by Theocritus, Idyll 24, "The Infant Hercules," and Idyll 17, in which Hercules is pictured seated at the table of the gods. Apollo was the patron god of the Julians, and Antony was descended from Hercules.

ECLOGUE V

This poem derives from Theocritus, Idylls 1, 6, and 7.

Codrus: Not identified, but the reference appears to be to a real or fictitious friend of the poet.

Daphnis: The name is from Theocritus's Idyll 1, where the story is quite different. But there are mythological stories about him more ancient than that, where he was an inventor of pastoral music.

thyrsus: The staff Bacchus carries.

Chios: A Greek island in the Aegean. The best wines came from there, and the very best from a region of the island called Ariusia.

Lyctian: Cretan.

Corydon loved the fair Alexis: See the first line of Eclogue II.

Whose flock is this? Is it Meliboeus's flock?: See the first line of Eclogue III.

ECLOGUE VI

The poem, which may be thought of as a kind of new beginning, the first poem in the second half of the book, shows signs of derivation from the Alexandrian poets Callimachus and Apollonius of Rhodes, not from Theocritus. The poem does declare that it (and the book) will go on playing the slender reed of pastoral, but here the songs that are described are those of the satyr Silenus. The "shepherd" who tells us about these songs is the poet himself, but Apollo, in the Latin text, calls him Tityrus.

Sicilian games: That is, the games Theocritus played.

Apollo / Tweaked my ear: Milton echoes Virgil's lines in "Lycidas."

how the seeds / of earth, and air, and water . . . : Virgil's sources are Apollonius's song of Orpheus and Lucretius's *De rerum natura*.

Proetus' maddened daughters: They were punished for mocking an image of Hera.

Dictaean Nymphs: Zeus was born on the mountain Dicte, in Crete.

Phaëton's sisters: Phaëton drove his horses too near the sun, and was killed. His sisters wept these tears grieving for him.

the king who married Procne: Tereus, who raped Philomela, his sister-in-law. Procne, his wife, and Philomela took vengeance by killing the little son of Tereus and Procne, and serving him as dinner to Tereus. Philomela was turned into a nightingale, Procne into a hoopoe.

ECLOGUE VII

burst with envy: Borrowed from "burst his guts," in Guy Lee's translation, *Virgil's Eclogues*.

the herbs / They grow in Sardinia: So bitter that people who eat them smile sardonic smiles.

The dedicatory passage of the poem is addressed to an important public figure who has recently returned, by way of the Adriatic Sea, from a military expedition abroad, and who has, apparently, written "Sophoclean" poetry. Traditionally this figure has been thought to be C. Asinius Pollio, who was a very powerful political figure, a general, a historian, and a writer of tragedy, and who had returned from such an expedition in 39 B.C.E. G. W. Bowersock and Wendell Clausen, however, have argued that the route described in the poem is implausible for him to have taken, but not implausible for Octavian (Augustus), who was engaged in a military expedition in the region of the Timavus in 35 B.C.E. The route of return from such a region would not be implausible. (And Octavian is said to have attempted to write a tragedy, on the subject of Ajax.)

Damon began his song: Damon's song derives from Theocritus, Idyll 3.

Love taught a mother how to stain her hands: The reference is to Medea, who, betrayed by Jason, killed their children.

Tityrus: Perhaps for "Tityrus" here we should read "Virgil," as in Eclogue VI.

. . . how Alphesiboeus replied: Alphesiboeus's song derives from Theocritus, Idyll 2.

Amaryllis: Here Amaryllis is the name of the servant of the woman whose song Alphesiboeus is singing.

ECLOGUE IX

"I own this place": Like Meliboeus, in Eclogue I, Moeris has been dispossessed, probably because his land has been given to a discharged veteran of Octavian's army. There is a Moeris also in Eclogue VIII.

so that your bees may avoid the Corsican yews: Corsica was famous for inferior honey.

Venus's grandson Caesar's star: A comet that appeared shortly after Julius Caesar's assassination.

The poems of Cornelius Gallus have been lost. This last of the Eclogues probably imitates passages from his *Amores*. The Eclogue derives also in some ways from Idylls of Theocritus and from the Alexandrian poet Callimachus.

I've called the speaker of the introductory passage (and the concluding lines) Virgil. But of course he both is and isn't wearing the mask of a shepherd in this final Eclogue.

What places do you now frequent, you Naiads: Milton imitates this passage (itself an imitation of Theocritus, Idyll 1) in "Lycidas." The passage beginning *The shepherds came, and after them the swineherds* is also echoed in "Lycidas."

Lycoris: A pseudonym used by Gallus for his beloved in his poems. Said to have been an actress whose stage name was Cytheris.

Glossary

ACHILLES: The foremost warrior of the Greeks against the Trojans, in the *Iliad*.

ADONIS: Son of Myrrha and her father Cinyras. Loved by Venus. He was slain by a wild boar. His blood became the anemone.

AGANIPPE: A fountain sacred to the Muses, at the foot of Mount Helicon in Greece.

ALCIDES: Hercules.

AMPHION: Son of Zeus and Antiope. A musician who built the walls of Thebes by means of his enchanting music.

ARACYNTHUS: A mountain in Attica, the region of Athens.

ARCADIA: A region of the Peloponnesus, in Greece; native region of Pan; the home country of pastoral song.

ARETHUSA: She was a nymph who was pursued by the Peloponnesian river Alpheus all the way to the harbor of Syracuse, in Sicily, where she became a fountain of pure water on an island.

ARGO: The ship the Argonauts sailed on, in search of the Golden Fleece.

ARION: Seventh century B.C.E. poet, said to have been saved from drowning by being carried ashore on the back of a dolphin.

ATALANTA: Atalanta had previously defeated her suitors in footraces, and then killed them. Hippomenes finally won her by distracting her, throwing the fabulous apples from the Garden of the Hesperides in front of her as she raced.

BACCHUS: The Roman name for Dionysus. God of wine, festivity, inspiration.

CALLIOPE: One of the Muses, the mother of Orpheus.

CANCER: The Crab; one of the zodiacal signs.

CERES: Goddess of agriculture. The Roman name for Demeter.

CINNA: A poet admired by Virgil; he was a friend of Catullus.

CIRCE: Enchantress who seduced Odysseus and gave his men a potion that turned them into swine. See Homer, *Odyssey*, X.

CONON: An Alexandrian mathematician and astronomer, third century B.C.E.

CREMONA: A town in the Po Valley which had suffered egregiously from Octavian's redistribution of land.

DELIA: The goddess Artemis, Diana, moon goddess, goddess of the hunt; born, like Apollo, on the island of Delos.

DRYADS: Wood nymphs.

EUROTAS: A Spartan river, the place where Apollo accidentally killed Narcissus, whom he loved.

GALLUS: Cornelius Gallus (69–26 B.C.E.). He was a greatly admired poet, most of whose work has been lost. He was a friend of Virgil's and he was a high public official in the regimes of Julius Caesar and Augustus. Some scholars have conjectured that Gallus's poems and their elaborate hypersophisticated style are echoed and imitated in Eclogue X, where Gallus is the lovelorn singer.

GARAMANTIAN DESERT: In the eastern Sahara, in Africa.

HEBRUS: A river in Thrace, in northern Greece.

HELICON: A mountain in Boeotia, in Greece, sacred to poetry, Apollo, the Muses.

HYBLA: A place in Sicily, famous for its honey.

ILLYRIA: A region across the Adriatic from Italy.

JOVE, JUPITER: Roman names for Zeus, head of the gods.

LINUS: A legendary poet, son of Apollo.

LUCINA: The Roman goddess of childbirth; in Roman mythology she became identified with Diana, the sister of Apollo.

LYCAEUS: The birthplace of Pan, in Arcadia.

MAECENAS: Gaius Maecenas (d. 8 B.C.E.). A wealthy adviser to Augustus and a patron of literature. Virgil and Horace belonged to his circle. He gave Horace his Sabine farm.

MAENALUS: A mountain sacred to Pan, in Arcadia.

MANTUA: The town near which Virgil was born.

MINCIUS: The river near Mantua, near Virgil's birthplace.

NAIADS: Water nymphs.

OCTAVIAN: The emperor Augustus, born C. Octavius (63 B.C.E.–C.E. 14), great-nephew of Julius Caesar.

ORPHEUS: Son of Apollo and the Muse Calliope. The greatest singer in the world.

PALES: Goddess of pastures and herds.

PALLAS: Athena, the patroness goddess of the city of Athens.

PAN: God of nature, flocks, shepherds, pastoral song.

PARCAE: The sister Fates.

PARIS: The son of Priam, later the seducer of Helen, was herdsman of his father's cattle on Mount Ida.

PARNASSUS: A mountain in central Greece, sacred to Apollo, the Muses, Dionysus.

PARTHENIUS: A mountain in Arcadia.

PARTHIAN: Parthia is a region in the Middle East, now Iran.

PIERIAN MAIDENS: The Muses (and Orpheus) were born at the Pierian spring in Greece.

PINDUS: A wild mountain range in Thrace.

POLLIO: C. Asinius Pollio (76 B.C.E.–C.E. 4), a general, statesman, historian, tragedian; a patron of Virgil's. Consul in 40 B.C.E. He built the first public library in Rome.

PONTUS: The Black Sea.

PRIAPUS: A god of procreation, whose ithyphallic statue was put up in gardens to guard them from mischief.

PYRRHA: The wife of Deucalion, who was the Noah of Greek mythology.

RHODOPE: A mountain in Thrace, in northern Greece.

SATURN: The Roman name for Cronus, father of Zeus, who overthrew and succeeded him. The age of Saturn is the Golden Age.

SCYLLA: A famous monster whirlpool in the sea between Italy and Sicily.

SCYTHIA: Vast region in Eurasia, from the Black Sea to the Aral Sea.

SILENUS: A satyr; tutor of Bacchus, god of wine and inspiration.

SYLVANUS: A god of the woods.

TIMAVUS: A river that empties into the northern Adriatic.

TMAROS: A mountain in Epirus, in Greece.

VARIUS: L. Varius Rufus, Virgil's friend and literary executor, a poet

and dramatist whom Virgil and Horace greatly admired. His works are lost.

VARUS: Publius Alfenus Varus. Consul in 39 B.C.E. One of the three (along with Pollio and Gallus) commissioners of Augustus overseeing the confiscation of lands (see the first and ninth Eclogues) for the purposes of rewarding war veterans. He may be the Varus to whom the sixth Eclogue is dedicated. (Some scholars argue that the dedicatee was a Roman general, Publius Quinctilius Varus. He committed suicide in 9 B.C.E., after his army was ambushed and decimated in Germany.)

VENUS: Roman name for Aphrodite, goddess of love.